The Self-Insurance Decision

by

Joseph M. Conder
Professor of Business Administration
Indiana University Southeast

and

Gilbert N. Hopkins
Associate Instructor
Indiana University, Bloomington

A study carried out on behalf of the
National Association of Accountants

Pubished by

National Association of Accountants
10 Paragon Drive, Montvale, NJ 07645
Copyright by National Association of Accountants © 1981
NAP Publication Number 81124
ISBN 0-86641-002-3

Table of Contents

Foreword

Every business enterprise is exposed to potential losses due to various possible events whose occurrence is not avoidable. For most types of loss exposure, the respective risks (chances of losses) are manageable through an insurance program. Prudent risk management seeks to maintain a sound balance between risk transfers (commercial insurance) and risk retention (self-insurance) in order to minimize the related expenses.

Financial data and analyses needed for risk management are provided mostly by accounting and financial managers. They also often participate in the decision process or are responsible for many of its phases. The study whose results are presented here was undertaken to help them perform these functions effectively, especially with respect to the self-insurance programs. We also hope that this report will be of interest to other people concerned with risk management, particularly in smaller companies.

The study findings show that a majority of American business enterprises self-insure a significant portion of the risks they face in the conduct of their operations. Self-insurance takes a variety of forms. Policy decisions on self-insurance are usually made by chief financial officers or chief executive officers. Specific self-insurance decisions then tend to be made by chief financial officers or insurance managers. For property and liability risks, larger firms rely more on self-insurance than smaller firms do. For employee-related risks, self-insuring is rather uniformly practiced by companies of various sizes.

Central in the research for this study was a mail survey of 400 randomly selected companies. Usable responses were received from 198 companies, a 49.5% response rate.

Highlights of findings and conclusions are presented in Chapter 1. A comprehensive description of self-insurance considerations, approaches, techniques and procedures is given in Chapter 2. The study method is covered in Chapter 3. Mail survey results are presented and analyzed in Chapters 4, 5 and 6. Summary and recommendations are in Chapter 7. The report also contains references to findings of previous studies (Appendix A), a case study (Appendix B), topical bibliography (Appendix C) and selected portions of an exposure inventory (Appendix D).

Guidance in the preparation of this research report was kindly and generously provided by the Project Committee:

Joseph J. McCann, Chairman
Ryan Homes, Inc.
Pittsburgh, Pa.

Richard F. Bebee
Alexander Grant & Company
Chicago, Ill.

Robert U. Boehman
North American Products, Inc.
Jasper, Ind.

Paul H. Levine
Magnetic Analysis Corporation
Mt. Vernon, N.Y.

The report reflects the views of the researchers and not necessarily those of the Association, the Committee on Research or the Project Committee.

Stephen Landekich
Research Director
National Association
of Accountants

Preface

This study was conceived and sponsored by the National Association of Accountants, principally for the edification of its members and their associates in the firms by which they are employed. As a result, we and the sponsor agreed at the outset that the study should stress the practical, as distinguished from the theoretical, aspects of self-insurance.

We wish to thank Stephen Landekich, research director of the National Association of Accountants, and the committee assigned responsibilities to oversee this project for their invaluable guidance and assistance. Especially does author Conder appreciate an extension of the project's deadline after he suffered a heart attack in the middle of the study. (Fortunately, he was not self-insuring his health care risks.)

Our special thanks are offered to the executives of the 198 companies who took time from their busy schedules to complete and return the questionnaire.

We also wish to acknowledge and express our appreciation to colleagues at Indiana University Southeast—Samuel E. Braden, Robert E. Osborn and Jerry E. Wheat—for generous consultative support, and to Paula Sylvester for typing the questionnaire and the manuscript of this publication.

Joseph M. Conder
New Albany, Ind.

Gilbert N. Hopkins
Bloomington, Ind.

Chapter 1

Introduction

Most business managers make insurance decisions at one time or another. Some of these decisions are made by full-time professional insurance managers, but many are made—or participated in—by managers whose day-to-day duties revolve around accounting, finance, production, personnel or some similar function and who only occasionally get involved in insurance decisions. It is to this latter group that we principally direct this publication.

As a part of its ongoing program of sponsoring research to benefit its members and the business community at large, the National Association of Accountants selected the study of self-insurance practices as a meaningful project. The NAA Committee on Research stated that it was "interested in examining the critical factors used by business and industry to evaluate the self-insurance decision." The prospectus continued, "The research should be focused on how the companies made the decision to self-insure, what the accounting treatment is for self-insured risks and how frequently and under what conditions the decision is re-evaluated."

The researchers listed many questions for which the findings might provide answers. Among the questions were:

1. What is self-insurance?
2. What is the background of self-insurance as an alternative to commercial insurance?
3. Who self-insures? Who self-insures the most?
4. Why was the decision made to self-insure or not to self-insure?
5. How has Financial Accounting Standards Board Statement No. 5, *Accounting for Contingencies,* affected the decision to self-insure?
6. How is a self-insurance program administered on a day-to-day basis?
7. What methods of funding are most prevalent?
8. How often is the self-insurance decision re-evaluated?
9. Which person makes self-insurance decisions?
10. What is the future of self-insurance as an alternative to commercial insurance?

The definitional and background phases of the research involved the customary review of pertinent literature, mainly those publications and articles referred to in Appendix A—Previous Studies and Appendix C—Topical Bibliography. Background information which was thought to be informative and interesting is included in the chapter titled "Is Self-Insurance for Your Company?"

The researchers and sponsor agreed that the best way to learn about current practices in self-insurance was to survey those businesses which are involved with self-insurance or have made a decision not to get involved. The researchers assumed that larger companies were more likely to have seriously considered the self-insurance alternative than smaller companies. Hence the survey was directed toward large publicly owned companies. (This is not meant to say that small companies must learn from large companies but, rather, that companies which have not seriously considered self-insurance should be able to learn from those which have.)

Results of the survey are contained in the chapters titled "The Questions and The Answers," "What the Answers Mean," and "Who Self-Insures the Most?"

Highlights of findings and conclusions of the research, listed in the same order as the questions originally posed by the researchers, are as follows:

1. Self-insurance takes a variety of forms ranging from a simple decision not to carry commercial insurance on a risk (or portion of a risk) to a company-owned "captive" insurance company to which premiums are paid.
2. Self-insurance, as an alternative to commercial insurance, has been around for many years and has been the subject of considerable writing and at least five studies prior to this one.
3. Most large companies are involved in some form of self-insurance. This generally is true across all lines of business.
4. The larger the company, the larger the percentage of its risks which are likely to be self-insured. Transportation and utility companies tend to be more heavily involved in self-insurance than those in other industries.
5. Factors influencing companies most in their self-insurance decisions, ranked according to prevalence, are:
   a) Financial capacity to stand loss,
   b) Qualified personnel to administer program,
   c) Emphasis on in-house loss prevention program,
   d) Geographic or similar dispersion of risks,
   e) Tying up funds in insurance premiums or deposits,
   f) Other factors affecting profitability.
6. Very few companies were heavily influenced by the Financial Accounting Standards Board prohibition of expense accruals in

financial statements for self-insurance. The same finding emerged with respect to the nondeductibility of such accruals for income tax purposes.

7. Most self-insurers calculate savings by comparing actual payments of losses and administrative costs over a period of time against previously quoted insurance premiums for the same period.

    Most self-insurers have no funding arrangement for expected losses—implying that they expect to cover self-insured losses from working capital.

    Most companies feel that it is necessary to account for administrative and claim costs as well as the actual losses in self-insured risks.

8. For those firms which fund for expected losses, separate bank accounts or securities are the most prevalent form.

9. The self-insurance decision is usually re-evaluated annually.

10. Policy decisions on self-insurance are usually made by the chief financial officer or the chief executive officer. Specific self-insurance decisions then tend to be made by the chief financial officer or the insurance manager.

11. More than half the firms now self-insuring expect to increase the practice in the next five years; fewer than half of the firms *not* now self-insuring foresee getting involved in the next five years.

The researchers have attempted to avoid bias for or against self-insurance. They have no desire to cause companies to enter into self-insurance arrangements, but they do want to cause managers to explore the possibilities fully. A well-intentioned business manager who is prudent yet alert to the possible advantages of risk-taking is the person to whom self-insurance may well be a viable business strategy.

Chapter 2

Is Self-Insurance for Your Company?

Few, if any, businesses are large enough or strong enough to withstand real calamities such as floods, fires or earthquakes. If there were even a remote possibility that such an event could "put it out of business," a company would attempt to become invulnerable. Perhaps it would consider moving or "running" from the potential calamity. If that weren't feasible, perhaps it could move a portion of its operations or facilities, thereby almost eliminating the possibility of total destruction. On a scale of 0 to 10, it is a lot easier to come back from 5 than from 0.

A firm's moving a portion of its facilities to another location is not a move into self-insurance, although it does help set the stage for at least a passing thought of the possibility of its risking a calamity at one location or the other. But we are getting ahead of ourselves. What we have here is a move toward loss prevention—or at least "total wipeout" prevention—which seems to be a logical move even if the firm has never heard of insurance or self-insurance.

Moving a portion of a firm's facilities may be looked at as a first step toward risk management. Even the best of loss prevention techniques cannot be expected to result in the avoidance of all risk. The best a company can hope for is to "manage" the risk of loss. This management might consist of purchasing every conceivable kind of coverage—with ultra-high limits—from commercial insurance carriers, or a company could decide to center its risk management completely in loss prevention measures without arranging for any outsider to help pay for losses not prevented. Prudent risk management can be expected to fall somewhere between these two extremes of lavish amounts of commercial insurance and plain no-insurance. In this study we wanted to find out where most businesses fit between the two extremes and, more particularly, *why* they have chosen that position. We hope the reasoning used by our respondents will be helpful to others in making more informed risk management decisions.

Risk[1] Identification

Any serious attempt at risk management begins—consciously or unconsciously—with risk identification. Whether a company uses an elaborate check list or uses a more intuitive approach, it needs to be aware of the potential losses it is exposed to before it can consider what to do about its exposure.

In a brainstorming type of risk identification session, company officials may draw up a long list of exposures to loss. Some of them, though quite real, do not lend themselves to being insured and are therefore outside the realm of the discussions in this publication. The following list is an example of loss exposures which would tend to be either insurable or noninsurable.

Insurable

Destruction of property by fire, tornado, and the like

Loss of profit resulting from foregoing destruction

Damage to property of others from negligence of our employee

Injury to employee from on-job accident

Illness of employee (when company has obligation to pay his costs of illness and/or continue his salary)

Injury or illness of customer resulting from use of our product

Noninsurable

Loss of profit from losing major customer

Loss of property by expropriation by foreign power

Cost of poor management decisions

Cost of workers' poor productivity

Required payments to shareholders for "failure to seize corporate opportunity"

Loss of profits from a competitor "outdoing" us

Violation of equal opportunity statutes

These lists are far from complete, but the discipline and thought processes used in drawing up such lists are the essence of risk identification. The list of

---

[1] Unless the context dictates otherwise, we shall use the term *risk* as we would expect business-people generally to use it—to mean "chance of loss." This usage differs from the insurance company's use of the term, where *risk* means the "variation between the expected incidence of loss and the actual incidence."

insurable loss exposures, expanded as appropriate, becomes the "case load" of the risk manager or person in the company who is responsible for minimizing losses from these types of events.

Again, risk management starts with risk identification—either conscious or unconscious. Those who do the best job of risk identification, of course, use a conscious, organized approach to the task. By and large, the focus should be on "things" and "people" which may get damaged or destroyed. Perhaps the intitial exposure list could be drawn up by following steps like these:[2]

1. Visual inspection of plants, warehouses, transportation facilities, offices and any other properties of the company
2. Visual inspection of the properties of contiguous neighbors
3. Examination of insurance policies in force
4. Summarization of loss history files
5. Review of contract files with customers, suppliers, and others
6. Examination of balance sheet accounts and detailed supporting ledgers
7. Review of labor contracts, workers' compensation laws, company benefit plans, and the like, dealing with the many rights of employees
8. Arrangement for an independent risk identification survey by an outsider such as an insurance agent, broker or consultant
9. Edit and formalize the lists prepared in the foregoing steps into one master list.

Following these steps will produce many duplications on the exposure list because the same buildings, for example, will be visually identified and found in ledgers. The idea is to identify, as nearly as possible, all potential items subject to loss. Duplications can be eliminated very easily in the edit routine and not present a problem. One additional thought with respect to risk identification: the people preparing the exposure lists should be cautioned not to omit a risk just because its occurrence is extremely unlikely. That judgment should be made later, during the process of wrestling with what to do about *all* of the identified risks.

Risk Quantification

After all conceivable exposures to loss have been listed, it is important to get into the question of *how much* exposure is present. Only after

---

[2] See, also, the "exposure inventory" in Appendix D.

attaching units or dollars to the exposure list is a company ready to tackle the decision-making phase of determining how to handle the various risks.

Quantification of risks can take several forms initially, leading ultimately to placing a dollar amount on each risk or combination of risks. Some risks lend themselves to direct "dollarization." An example would be the destruction by fire of the merchandise inventory of a convenience store, whose home office keeps a running inventory record, at both cost and retail, of the merchandise in each of its stores. The primary purpose of such record, of course, is not for determining how much insurance to carry or how much not to carry.[3] But insurance managers are a resourceful lot and utilize any record they can find which will serve their purpose.

Among the risks for which dollar figures are readily available are the following:

1) *Inventories of all types.* You can't always get an instant dollar figure for an inventory, but you really don't need an actual inventory amount unless you suffer an actual loss. In planning how to handle risk of loss, you can focus on "normal" inventory amounts which may be plotted from accounting record balances of the past three or four fiscal year-ends. If the business has a distinct seasonal pattern, you may need to superimpose the monthly pattern onto the graph in order to get a better idea of what the high and low inventory balances might run during the upcoming year.[4]

2) *Plant and equipment.* Again, the accounting records should show dollar costs for the various buildings, machines, vehicles, and the like listed during the risk identification procedure. Because of inflation, however, acquisition cost figures are probably well under the amounts which would be needed to replace such items in the event of loss. It is necessary, therefore, to devise a scheme for bringing the costs up-to-date. You can use vendors' catalogs, vendors' quotations, recent costs of similar items, cost of living or construction cost indexes, engineers' appraisals or some other method. In some companies, much of this work will already have been done in order to comply with "current cost" or "replacement cost" requirements of the Financial Accounting Standards Board or the Securities and Exchange Commission. As with inventories, it is important that separate dollar figures be accumulated for each location subject to a common fire or other similar event.

---

[3] The major reason for keeping the convenience store's book inventory figures updated on a daily basis, incidentally, is to facilitate surprise audits. The auditor, who may be the manager of another store, can add up the retail price of all the stock in a few hours and compare his total with the home office figure, via telephone, as soon as he finishes counting.

[4] If the identification list did not show each inventory location separately, it should be done during the quantification phase. You get quite a different "feel" of exposure when you have $100 million inventory in one building as compared with the chain of convenience stores with $100,000 in each of 1,000 stores. The latter situation is what might be termed a "natural" for self-insurance.

3) *Cash and securities.* Companies with substantial amounts of extremely liquid assets must be concerned about theft or misappropriation as well as the peril of fire. If you are speaking of assets *owned* by the company, both cost and current-value dollar amounts should be available from the balance sheet and supporting detailed ledgers. If the assets are held in a custodial role—safe deposit vault of bank, public warehouse, consignments in, and armored car service, as examples—it will be necessary to obtain dollar amounts from the owners of such assets. (This is easy to say but may be hard to accomplish. How does a bank, for example, arrive at even a "ball park estimate" of the dollar value of the contents of its safe deposit boxes when customers are afforded absolute privacy in access to the boxes?)

More often than not, dollar figures are not so readily available, and potential losses must first be quantified in some other unit with dollars, or dollar estimates, to be attached later. Examples of these types of situations follow:

1) *Employee accidents.* Many companies that carefully evaluate their potential losses to physical assets make no attempt to estimate the future impact of employee accidents. Granted that you are getting into a more subjective area, you may not be content to turn the whole problem over to the insurance company. A study of the number of accidents and the dollar amount of awards during the most recent three-year period should provide an adequate base period from which to estimate one year forward. If such information is not readily available in the company files, it should be easily obtainable from the insurer or other organization handling the company's workers' compensation claims. (Please bear in mind that, while it is harder to get a handle on the number of dollars at risk with employee accidents than with inventories, it is easier to predict the pattern of occurrence because worker accidents happen much more often than fires.)

2) *Liability.* Quantification of potential dollar losses from damage to the property or persons of nonemployees would follow the same lines as for workers' compensation. The frequency and severity of "slips and falls" on the company premises, illnesses from consumption of company products, damages inflicted by company vehicles, and other such accidents may be predicted by averaging the most recent three to five years. Estimating the dollar amount of awards is much more difficult, however, than for employee accidents. While workers' compensation awards vary between states, they tend to be standard within each state for each type of injury. For example, loss of a forefinger may result in an award of $200 per week for 12 weeks, or $2,400, regardless of whether the employee returns to work in 12 weeks or six weeks. Awards in liability cases, on the other hand, are anything but standard since they are usually set by juries. Also, in certain situations, the suit is filed as a class action with the possibility of awards to thousands of unknown persons. (False or misleading financial representations by corporate officials or public accountants might be an example of such a situation.)

3) *Employee benefits.* Conceptually, the contracting of pneumonia by the child of an employee is not a risk of the company. Over the years, though, employers have taken on more and more of this risk. The company's obligation may be contractual—as with a labor union—or merely an

announced or implicit company policy. In any event, the liability for most companies is substantial and needs to be estimated in order to complete the risk exposure picture, preparatory to getting into decisions of what to do about the various risks. Short of epidemics which, fortunately, have been almost nonexistent in recent years, the incidence and dollar cost of health care claims probably are easier to estimate than the others previously discussed. (An admonition would be to not forget to add 10% to 20% to last year's dollar amounts for the spiraling pattern of doctors' and hospitals' bills.)

Risk Handling

We struggled a bit before using the term "handling" to head this section of our comments. Another possibility was "risk management," but that term has a broader connotation to include risk identification and risk quantification. We also considered "risk treatment" but concluded that sounds too medicinal. We are not sure that anyone can claim to be able to actually *handle* risks; what we wish to discuss in this section are the various possibilities available to the company in *attempting* to handle the risks that have been identified and quantified.

Faced with the possibility or probability of losses resulting from various types of accidents, acts of nature or similar incidents, the very first tactic which occurs to the business manager should be *avoidance*. Full avoidance rarely is a viable approach, however, because it means conducting the business in such a way as not to expose it to the particular type of loss being considered. Avoidance might call for such a radical change in the company's operations that there would be too many offsetting disadvantages. There may be occasional opportunities for making a choice where one alternative would provide virtual avoidance. A Texas electric utility, for example, could opt for constructing its new generating station 100 miles from the Gulf of Mexico rather than adjacent to the Gulf—in order to avoid a hurricane loss. The trade-off in this case might be that it would not be able to receive coal deliveries by barge and would have to pay higher rail charges. The utility also might decide to go underground with its transmission lines after losing a lawsuit growing out of a plane's crashing after running afoul of lines attached to poles. The company would avoid another "air" accident but might encounter some other kind of problem in digging up the countryside.

If the company cannot come up with a feasible way of avoiding exposure to a loss, it should try loss *prevention* or reducing the likelihood of an actual occurrence. Prevention measures should be instituted regardless of what decision a company makes about self-insurance, but there appears to be a stronger motive for a prevention program for a company which isn't carrying commercial insurance on a particular risk. Examples of prevention programs followed by many companies are shown on the next page.

Employee accidents and sickness:
- Plant safety programs relating to use of equipment
- Good housekeeping procedures
- Company-sponsored exercise program
- Alcoholic, drug and other counseling programs
- Preventive maintenance programs

Fire and similar damages:
- Sprinkler system
- Fireproof doors and construction materials
- Separation of operations into several buildings (when it is feasible)
- Auxiliary water supply
- Security systems (alarm, watchmen, and the like)

Theft:
- Security systems (alarms, watchmen, and the like)
- Private detective "plants" (stores, factories and offices)

Liability:
- Improved product design, packaging and labeling
- Improved physical layout of store buildings, escalators and such used by the public

In recent years, loss exposures resulting from accidents to employees, customers and the general public have been highlighted by new federal legislation. The Occupational Safety and Health Administration (OSHA) and the Consumer Product Safety Commission (CPSC) have been quite visible to many businesspeople. While neither OSHA nor CPSC has won any popularity contests, they probably have had some beneficial results in loss prevention. There are many corrective actions taken as a result of OSHA inspections, and some reduction in employee accidents should follow. Also, there have been significantly increased expenditures for employee safety and health equipment, according to a McGraw-Hill study, and, again, some prevention of loss should result.

While government agencies may serve as catalysts in companies' loss prevention programs, it remains the responsibility of insurance managers, safety directors and line executives to stay alert to the possibilities of reducing the frequency or severity of the various accidents that are likely to occur in the day-to-day operations of their companies.

Even though a company does its best to avoid or prevent losses, many probably will still occur. How then will the organization "handle" the cost of medical treatment for the injured employee, replacement of the burned warehouse, or other disaster? The two general approaches available are *transfer* and *retention*. By "transfer" we mean, generally, paying a premium to an insurance company and contractually transferring to the insurance company the obligation to pay the injured employee's medical bills or pay for the reconstruction of the burned warehouse. "Retention" means that the company itself will stand loss. The company may be able to soften the impact of the loss by a spreading device such as systematically setting aside money into a self-insurance fund, paying regular premiums to an owned (captive) insurance company, banding together with competitors in loss-sharing arrangements, or other similar devices. These methods are also "retention" techniques because there is no outsider who is "on the hook" to get your company "off the hook."

Frequently the company employs a combination *transfer/retention* arrangement. The most common of these arrangements is the deductible clause built into many, if not most, commercial insurance policies. By increasing the size of the deductible from a minimal amount to a truly significant amount,[5] the company is practicing retention, or self-insurance, by assuming the first "layer" of loss. If the company is prepared to assume a larger portion of loss, it can purchase "stop loss," "umbrella" or similar commercial insurance policies which will take care of the last layer of loss. Most companies will seldom, if ever, have to call upon the insurer in these latter arrangements, but they have the comfort of knowing someone is standing by in the event of a catastrophic loss.

Retention of risk is what this study is about—with emphasis on the question of how and why companies decide for or against retaining risk—or self-insuring. The forms of self-insurance focused on in this study, and which 400 randomly selected public companies were asked to focus on while completing the questionnaire, are these:

1) *Large deductibles in commercial policies.* (A clause in the contract with the insurance company which states that it will be responsible only for the portion of loss which exceeds a specific amount.) Deductibles are the most common type of self-insurance insofar as property and liability coverages are involved. In most instances the selection of the size of the deductible largely is intuitive. A financial officer or insurance manager will look at the current premium of a policy with a $1,000 deductible and ask, "How much smaller will the premium be if we increase the deductible to $10,000 or perhaps $100,000?" He then may make a completely subjective decision, saying to himself or to one of his colleagues, "We have collected very little over the years on this policy. I believe we can chance raising the deductible in order to reduce the premium." In other instances, the approach to increasing deductibles is more structured and objective, similar to that followed in devising a self-insurance program.

---

[5] For the purposes of our study we arbitrarily selected 10% of coverage as the point at which a deductible would be classified as self-insurance. The reader may prefer to use some other percentage or a specified dollar amount.

2) *Self-insurance program.* (An organized, active plan to absorb certain losses rather than transfer the risk to a commercial insurance company. The number of dollars to be absorbed may be limited by purchasing a "stop loss" policy or an "excess coverage" policy. Anticipated self-insured losses may or may not be provided for in advance by funding arrangements.) When firms are faced with large insurance premiums and with the understanding that perhaps only 50% to 70% of premiums are paid out in loss claims by commercial insurance companies, it is natural that they consider turning to their own self-insurance programs.

Professor Mark R. Greene has listed five requirements a firm should meet before really getting serious about its own self-insurance program:[6]

1. The firm has a sufficient number of objects so situated that they are not subject to simultaneous destruction. The objects are also reasonably homogeneous in nature and value so that calculations as to probable losses will be accurate within a narrow range. If these conditions are present, the firm will be able to predict accurately the size of fund necessary to meet the losses expected.

2. Management is willing to set aside a fund to meet the large and unusual losses. Until the fund is built up, normally a program of outside commercial insurance must be maintained. As the size of the self-insurance fund increases, the amount of outside insurance can be reduced and finally eliminated. It is not satisfactory to have merely a "book" reserve for this purpose since such a balance sheet transaction would not provide the cash if the loss were to occur. The fund must be actually set aside from operating assets and invested in securities that can be readily convertible into cash should the need arise. If a firm feels that a separate fund is not required, that it can meet any losses out of working capital, then it is not using self-insurance but is simply assuming the risk—or using noninsurance.

3. The firm must have accurate records or have access to satisfactory statistics to enable it to make good estimates of the expected loss, otherwise it is guessing at the size of the necessary fund and has not successfully handled the risk of loss. To increase the accuracy of the calculations, it is wise to use data over as long a period as possible, not merely the last five or 10 years. If outside data are used, it is necessary to exercise extreme caution to see that the data employed are applicable to the firm's own experience.

4. The general financial condition of the firm should be satisfactory. There is a tendency for business persons who are in financial difficulties to believe that self-insurance is a good way to save on insurance. While it is often true that the firm can save money by self-insuring, it is possible only when all of the preceding conditions are met. If a firm is in financial straits, it is unlikely that the necessary fund will be set aside or that if it is set aside it will be of sufficient size to meet the risk. If the firm cannot afford insurance premiums, it is even more unlikely that the firm can afford the loss should it occur or that the firm can afford to set aside a self-insurance fund.

---

[6] Mark R. Greene, *Risk and Insurance,* 4th Ed. (Southwestern, 1977).

5. The self-insurance plan requires careful administration and planning. Someone has to be in charge of investing the self-insurance fund, paying claims, inspecting exposures, preventing losses, keeping necessary records, and performing the many other duties connected with any insurance program. If the necessary specialized executive talent is not available, and if the business cannot appreciate the necessity of paying continuing attention to all the details of carry-through, self-insurance will not be a satisfactory solution.

While the last four of these criteria are rather general in nature, the first should be applied to specific risks to assess whether your company should consider a self-insurance program. If you are focusing on the possibility of destruction of buildings by fire, you are not a very good candidate for a self-insurance program if you have only one building (a bank, for example). On the other hand, a chain of 1,000 company-owned fast food restaurants may be an excellent candidate—if it meets the other four requirements. With respect to liability actions, perhaps an automobile manufacturer would self-insure its exposure. (A case such as the Indiana criminal case against Ford for rear-end explosions in its Pinto could influence this decision.) In the cases of workers' compensation and employee health care and other benefits—or "people insurance"—most firms have a sufficient number of homogeneous objects to seriously consider self-insuring.[7]

Before leaving this discussion of self-insurance programs, we should add a sixth requirement cited by most writers—that the firm provide for catastrophe protection against losses greater than those it is willing or able to absorb. Such protection might be afforded by an "umbrella" policy, a "stop loss" policy, or an "excess coverage" policy.

3) *Captive insurance company.* (A form of self-insurance in which a company purchases regular commercial coverage from an insurance company it owns. For the purposes of this study the "captive" may be owned by several companies so long as it does not sell insurance to nonowners. To the extent that the captive reinsures risk with others, such reinsurance is considered commercial insurance for the purposes of this study.) Captives are by no means a new phenomenon, dating at least to 1900. They have become more and more popular with self-insuring firms, however. It is estimated that there are currently at least 1,000 firms funneling a significant portion of their insurance premium dollars into an insurance company subsidiary. A large part of these dollars do not remain in the captives but go out to commercial insurance companies through reinsurance arrangements. In effect, the captive can "get it wholesale" for its parent. This idea is not unlike having a captive travel agency or captive advertising agency in order to save the 10% - 15% commissions that go for those services. We do not mean to leave the impression that captive insurance companies cannot or do not

---

[7]The "mass and homogeneity" requirement is no different, in concept or in operation, for self-insurance than for commercial insurance. The only requirement is that you must have a sufficient quantity of objects for the law of large numbers to operate within your own company in the case of self-insurance, whereas the commercial insurance company can combine the objects of many companies in order to accumulate a sufficient quantity.

retain the risk-absorbing function. The amount of loss a captive can cover depends, of course, on the size of its initial capitalization, its maturity, and its loss experience to date.

4) *No insurance*. (A passive situation where the company simply doesn't purchase commercial insurance or enter into a self-insurance program.) Purists may protest the inclusion of "no insurance" as a form of self-insurance. Goshay proposed this definition:[8] *Self-insurance is the conscious retention of risk, the level of which has been limited within the financial capacity of the firm, emanating from a distribution of exposures which permit reasonable predictions as to future loss probabilities.* We do not argue with his definition, but we submit that many business managers commit their firms to risk retention without making precise, scientific predictions of future loss probabilities. Even those who responded in this study that they considered it necessary to maintain complete and accurate loss records may not be using those records to formally predict the future.

Practiced with discretion, we believe that the simple expedient of not insuring certain *known* risks is a very straightforward form of self-insurance—not always appropriate—but straightforward. Those of us who consider ourselves to be good drivers, and omit collision coverage from our auto insurance, are practicing some very basic, "close to home" self-insurance.

We hope that this chapter has motivated you to look further into self-insurance for your firm (or look into further self-insurance, if you are already self-insuring). Specifically, we hope you will study the remaining chapters of the publication so that you can learn from the reported experiences of the 198 respondents to the questionnaire used in our study.

---

[8]Robert C. Goshay, *Corporate Self-Insurance and Risk Retention Plans,* p. 21 (Irwin, 1964).

Chapter 3

The Study Method

The findings of this study are based upon responses from 198 large public companies in a mail survey of 400 such companies.

Data Collection

Mail surveys, telephone surveys and personal interviews are commonly employed methods of collecting the types of data needed for this study. Because we wanted information from business firms in many areas of the country and because the questions to be asked were fairly numerous and complex, we designed a mail survey so respondents would have ample time for thoughtful answers.

To obtain information which was believed to be pertinent to the self-insurance decision, the researchers developed 26 questions which are reproduced, together with tabulations of responses, in "The Questions and the Answers" chapter.

The questionnaire was designed to elicit "what" and "why" answers from all respondents and "how" answers from those who self-insure. Before finalization, the questionnaire was field-tested in three companies where the researchers had personal contacts. We appreciate the contribution of the officials of these companies, none of which was included in the 400-company sample.

The Sample

There are many lists of firms available. Examples of sources for such lists are Dun & Bradstreet, U.S. Bureau of the Census, Moody's, and Standard and Poor's. We chose Standard and Poor's COMPUSTAT® lists for two reasons. First, we had direct computer access to the information maintained in the COMPUSTAT® data base. Second, we decided that the information we sought could be obtained best from publicly held firms since (a) they tend to be larger and, presumably, more likely to have considered self-insuring than would have smaller firms, and (b) they are accustomed to providing information to the public. The COMPUSTAT® lists of companies were compact and numerically oriented, which helped to simplify the selection of a sample. All companies contained in their lists are publicly owned.

We selected 400 companies at random from the 3,341 companies comprising the COMPUSTAT® Industrial Annual and Quarterly file and the COMPUSTAT® OTC Industrial Annual file, exclusive of insurance companies.[1] Based on the two-digit Standard Industrial Classification Index, the 3,341 companies were distributed as follows among the various major industrial groups:

	No.	%
Agriculture, forestry, and fishing	18	.5
Mining	171	5.1
Construction	48	1.4
Manufacturing	1,836	55.1
Transportation, communication, electric, gas, and sanitary services	324	9.7
Wholesale and retail trade	435	13.0
Finance and real estate	260	7.8
Services	228	6.8
Conglomerates	21	.6
	3,341	100.0%

While these companies are not necessarily representative of all U.S. businesses, we believe that they are fairly representative of larger publicly owned companies. Because the 400 subject companies were randomly selected, we made no analysis of their distribution among industrial groups prior to mailing. An analysis of the industry class of the companies who returned completed questionnaires—shown elsewhere in this monograph—matches rather well with the industry distribution of the population shown above. The most significant differences were that mining was underrepresented and the transportation, communications and utility group was overrepresented among our respondents.

We received usable responses from 198 companies after two follow-up mailings—one by postcard and one by letter. The response rate was 49.5%, rather typical for studies of this type.

Statistical Analysis

The questionnaire primarily sought "nominal" data. For example, we

---

[1] It might have been interesting to study how commercial insurance companies handle their own risk management practices. We decided, however, to omit them from this study in the belief that their practices would tend to be atypical.

asked the person completing the questionnaire to indicate his or her title. In order to tabulate these responses, we assigned numerical labels such as "1," "2," "3," and so on, The fact that the response "insurance manager" received the label "4" and "controller" received the label "5," however, does not mean "insurance manager" is equal to 4/5 "controller" or that "controller" is equal to 5/4 "insurance manager." Thus, these are nominal or "in name only" groupings.

Many statistical techniques are not appropriate for analyzing nominal data. (To find the *average* title, for example, is nonsensical.) In the main, we have utilized two statistical tools—frequency tables and cross tabulations— in this study. Frequency tables are used in "The Questions and the Answers" chapter and cross tabulation tables in most of the other chapters.

A frequency table is simply a list of all possible responses to a given question and the number or percentage of respondents choosing a particular answer. We have chosen to present percentages as they tend to be meaningful to the reader in analyzing a table.

A simple cross tabulation table is a combination of two frequency tables. The result is a single table showing one variable on the vertical axis and another variable on the horizontal axis. This effort aids in determining whether the two variables are related—one affecting the other—or are independent—neither affecting the other.

For example, if out of 200 respondents there are 100 controllers and 100 insurance managers, we would obtain the following frequency table.

EXAMPLE 1
Title of Respondent

Controller	100
Insurance manager	100
Total	200

Now, if we construct a cross tabulation of title with size of firm where we know 100 of the firms are of size "1" and 100 are of size "2," we would expect the following results if the position of the person completing the questionnaire is independent of the size of the firm:

EXAMPLE 2

	Size of Firm		
	1	2	
Controller	50	50	100
Insurance manager	50	50	100
	100	100	

Examination of the table shows that firms of both sizes were just as likely to assign completion of the questionnaire to the controller as to the insurance manager. Or, we might obtain these frequencies:

EXAMPLE 3

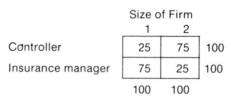

	Size of Firm		
	1	2	
Controller	25	75	100
Insurance manager	75	25	100
	100	100	

These data indicate that for size "2" firms, completion of the questionnaire was three times more likely to be assigned to the controller than to the insurance manager. (It also indicates, of course, that insurance managers completed the questionnaire in most of the small firms.) The implication is that these two variables—title of person completing questionnaire and size of firm—are associated.

Knowing that a relationship exists in a *sample* of a larger group of firms, however, does not guarantee a similar relationship in the entire larger group (population). In the case of each cross tabulation, we need somehow to determine how sure we can be that the relationship we see in the table actually exists in the real world. Or, alternatively, what is the probability that the relationship observed in the sample resulted from the sample not being representative of the population (that is, resulted from sampling error)? We used the Chi-square statistical testing procedure extensively to test the independence between variables which we had decided might have a significant association. We have shown the Chi-square test results below most of the tables.[2] When the test showed doubt about the independence of the variables (i.e., a 5% chance that the result is caused by sampling error rather than relationship between the variables), we frequently commented upon the fact. As is customary with data of the type we are handling, it was necessary to collapse certain tables in order to meet required minimum expected responses per cell.[3] In combining rows or columns containing small numbers of responses, we attempted to combine variables which we believe have similar attributes.

---

[2] Results of the Chi-square tests show a significance level expressed as a decimal fraction, or percentage. A small percentage approaching 0.0 indicates a strong likelihood of relationship, or association, between the variables. A large percentage approaching 1.0 indicates a strong likelihood of independence between the variables and a strong possibility that the differences in the observed frequencies resulted from sampling error.

[3] Chi-square tests are unreliable when more than 20% of the cells have expected frequencies smaller than 5 or when any cell has an expected frequency smaller than 1. (Sidney Siegel, *Nonparametric Statistics for the Behavioral Science*, McGraw-Hill, 1956, p. 110.)

Chapter 4

The Questions and the Answers

This chapter includes all the questions asked in the questionnaire and the responses to the questions. Because the convenience of the respondent took precedence over the convenience of the researchers and the readers in the design of the questionnaire, it is not duplicated precisely here except for the introductory page. Rather, we have reproduced the questions verbatim with the responses arranged for the convenience of the reader.

The respondent was permitted to check multiple answers to many of the questions. In others, only a single response was permitted. In both cases, responses have been presented as a percentage of total rather than as the number of valid answers. Where multiple responses were permitted, columns show no total. Where only one answer was permitted, columns add to 100%. Where meaning and clarity gain, we rank responses by magnitude rather than presenting them in the order of choices offered the respondents.

The questionnaire was designed in a three-part format:

1. The first 11 questions were asked of self-insurers and non-self-insurers to elicit information about when, how, why, and by whom the decision is made to commercially insure or to self-insure. The number of respondents was 198.
2. The next nine questions were asked only of self-insurers in order to gain insight into how they deal with the "nuts and bolts" aspects of self-insurance. There were 142 self-insurers in the group of 198 respondents.
3. The last part had as its purpose the accumulation of classification data such as type of business, size, and the like.

The survey questionnaire begins on the next page.

Self-Insurance Survey
Information Questionnaire

Introduction

Indiana University, under a grant from the National Association of Accountants, is collecting information about how businesses decide how to handle their risk management activities. Some companies use commercial insurance only, while others use commercial insurance, insurance with large deductibles, self-insurance programs, captive insurance companies, and/or, in some instances, no insurance.

In order to learn how decisions are made in this important area, we are asking a randomly selected group of companies to complete the following questionnaire. Your responses will be held confidential; all the data will be analyzed on a group basis in order to assist companies interested in pursuing the self-insurance option.

Thank you for your help.

General Definition

"Self-insurance" has a broad meaning in this questionnaire. In essence, it covers all methods of handling the risk of loss other than covering 100% of risk with purchased commercial insurance. The forms of self-insurance which will be frequently referred to in the questionnaire are:

1) *Large deductibles in commercial policies* (We have arbitrarily chosen 10% of risk as the minimum deductible which we will consider to be self-insurance. In other words, if you are required to absorb the first $100,000 of loss on a building worth $950,000, you are self-insuring, for the purposes of this study.)

2) *Self-insurance program* (An organized, active plan to absorb certain losses rather than transfer the risk to a commercial insurance company. The number of dollars to be absorbed may be limited by purchasing a "stop loss" policy or an "excess coverage" policy. Anticipated self-insured losses may or may not be provided for in advance by funding arrangements.)

3) *Captive insurance company* (A form of self-insurance in which a company purchases regular commercial coverage from an insurance company which it owns. For the purposes of this study the "captive" may be owned by several companies so long as it does not sell insurance to nonowners. To the extent that the captive reinsures risk

with others, such reinsurance is considered commercial insurance for the purposes of this study.)

4) *No insurance* (A passive situation where the company simply doesn't purchase commercial insurance or enter into a self-insurance program. While not technically self-insurance, this category has been included in the questionnaire in an attempt to cover all risk management possibilities.)

1. Who makes the policy decision in your organization to insure or self-insure risks?

Chief financial officer	32.2%
Chief executive	25.5
Insurance manager	12.2
Finance—executive committee	9.2
Insurance manager and others	7.7
Board of directors	7.1
Other	2.0
No policy decision	4.1
	100.0%

2. Who makes the specific decision as to insuring or self-insuring a specific risk?

A financial officer	39.3%
Insurance manager	36.7
Finance—executive committee	5.6
Insurance manager and others	5.6
An accounting officer	1.0
Other	8.2
No specific decision	3.6
	100.0%

3. When do you *usually* decide between handling risks by purchase of commercial insurance or by one of the self-insurance techniques?

When commercial policies expire	38.2%
When risks are first identified	34.6
When new risks occur	10.6
One-time decision which becomes standing policy	9.0
Other	4.9
No decision actually made	2.7
	100.0%

4. Will you please check the appropriate boxes to indicate how your company is handling the following types of risks? (Check as many boxes as are applicable.)

	Commercial Insurance	Large Deductibles (more than 10% of risk)	Self-Insurance Program	Captive Insurance Company	No Insurance
Property:					
Buildings	96.0%	21.2%	7.1%	4.0%	5.6%
Machinery & equipment	95.5	23.2	8.6	4.5	5.6
Inventories	87.4	21.7	9.1	3.5	7.6
Business interruption	78.8	17.2	6.6	2.5	18.2
Other	13.1	3.5	5.6	1.5	2.0
Liability:					
General (premises and operations)	86.9	19.7	14.6	6.6	1.5
Products	78.3	16.7	11.6	6.6	5.6
Auto	87.4	20.2	14.1	5.1	1.0
Other	11.6	3.0	3.5	1.0	1.0
Workers' compensation	72.2	8.6	36.4	3.5	1.5
Employee benefits:					
Basic health	72.7	4.0	28.3	.5	0.0
Major medical	73.7	4.5	27.3	.5	0.0
Life	92.4	4.5	5.1	.5	0.0
Disability	75.8	4.5	18.7	.5	5.6

5. What percent of your total insurable risk do you estimate is being self-insured by your company through large deductibles, self-insurance programs, captive insurance companies, and/or "no insurance?" (Check one box for each type of risk. We understand that some of the estimates may be "rough.")

	None	1% to 25%	26% to 50%	51% to 99%	100%
Property:					
Buildings	26.4	64.2	4.1	2.6	2.6
Machinery &					
equipment	25.9	64.2	5.2	2.1	2.6
Inventories	26.5	61.9	2.2	4.4	5.0
Business interruption	25.8	50.0	7.9	4.5	11.8
Other	15.4	41.0	7.7	10.3	25.6
Liability:					
General (premises					
and operations)	39.2	37.1	10.3	10.8	2.6
Products	39.2	34.3	10.5	9.9	6.1
Auto	39.1	38.5	10.4	8.3	3.6
Other	19.2	46.2	11.5	11.5	11.5
Workers' compensation	43.9	18.0	6.9	22.8	8.5
Employee benefits:					
Basic health	52.1	13.3	2.1	16.0	16.5
Major medical	51.9	14.8	2.1	15.9	15.3
Life	76.5	12.3	3.2	5.9	2.1
Disability	57.5	16.7	5.9	6.5	13.4

25

6. Of your company's *total* self-insured risk, what percent do you estimate is being handled by each of these means? (Please state your answers in round percentages ending in "0" such as 10%, 20%, etc. Your answers should add to 100%.)

Large deductibles (more than 10% of risk)	31 %
Self-insurance program	53 %
Captive insurance company	6 %
No insurance	10 %
Total	100 %
Not applicable—no self-insurance	0 %

The percentages shown above are arithmetic averages of the answers. The following table is a compilation of the actual answers.

	Percentage of Respondents Using These Means to Extent Shown in First Column			
Percentage Handled*	Large Deductibles (more than 10% of risks)	Self-Insurance Program	Captive Insurance Company	No Insurance
0	46.1	35.6	87.0	71.2
10	10.5	11.0	3.7	15.2
20	13.6	7.3	1.0	5.2
30	2.6	3.1	2.1	2.1
40	3.1	3.7	1.6	.5
50	2.1	4.2	.5	2.1
60	1.6	1.6	1.0	1.6
70	5.2	3.1	2.1	0.0
80	4.7	7.9	1.0	0.0
90	4.2	9.9	0.0	.5
100	6.3	12.6	0.0	1.6
	100.0%	100.0%	100.0%	100.0%

*In the few instances when respondents' answers were not stated in percentages ending in "0," they were rounded downward.

7. Please indicate how much influence the following factors have played in your decision(s) to self-insure or not to self-insure, regardless of when the decision was made.

	Heavy Influence	Some Influence	No Influence	Total
Financial capacity to withstand losses	79.1%	19.4%	1.5%	100.0%
Qualified personnel to administer program	29.5	50.5	20.0	100.0
Geographic or similar dispersion of risks	28.8	41.8	29.4	100.0
Emphasis on in-house loss-prevention program	25.7	49.7	24.6	100.0
Nonavailability of commercial insurance	8.9	24.6	66.5	100.0
Nonaffordability of commercial insurance	13.6	33.5	52.9	100.0
Loading (profit) included in commercial premiums	18.4	37.4	44.2	100.0
Tying up funds in commercial premiums and/or deposits	26.3	43.2	30.5	100.0
Other factors affecting your profitability	10.5	52.5	37.0	100.0
Predisposition of chief or other top executive	11.1	30.5	58.4	100.0
Nondeductibility for tax purposes of self-insurance accruals	6.3	38.7	55.0	100.0
Financial Accounting Standards Board prohibition against self-insurance accruals	6.9	30.9	62.2	100.0

8. How do you identify the insurable risks which your company faces? (Check as many boxes as are applicable.)

	Property	Liability	Workers' Compensation	Employee Benefits
Balance sheet analysis	54.5%	28.8%	15.2%	12.1%
Check list— developed internally	52.0	51.0	46.5	43.4
Check list— developed externally	18.2	17.2	15.7	13.1
Analysis by outside consultant, broker or insurance company	54.0	56.1	53.0	54.5
Other	13.1	14.6	13.6	10.1

9. How do you estimate the potential dollar magnitude of risks?

Informal determination based on judgment and experience	36.4%
Various informal and formal studies	23.1
Loss probability study performed internally	22.1
Loss probability study performed by outside consultant, broker or insurance company	12.3
Assets shown on balance sheet	5.1
Other	1.0
	100.0%

10. Is your company likely to increase or decrease the use of self-insurance in the next five years?

	Property	Liability	Workers' Compensation	Employee Benefits
Increase	59.2%	61.2%	51.8%	58.9%
Decrease	1.0	1.6	1.0	1.6
Neither	39.8	37.2	47.2	39.5
Total	100.0%	100.0%	100.0%	100.0%

11. How often do you re-evaluate your prior decision to insure or self-insure risks?

	Property	Liability	Workers' Compensation	Employee Benefits
Annually	45.4%	49.2%	45.3%	38.2%
As circumstances change	34.5	35.2	33.4	41.9
Within 2 - 5 years	14.4	9.4	13.0	11.0
Not consciously done	5.7	6.2	8.3	8.9
	100.0%	100.0%	100.0%	100.0%

*   *   *   *   *   *   *   *   *   *   *

IF YOUR COMPANY IS NOT SELF-INSURING (i.e., IF YOU DID NOT CHECK ANY BOX IN THE LAST FOUR COLUMNS OF QUESTION 4) PLEASE SKIP THE REMAINING NUMBERED QUESTIONS AND COMPLETE THE CLASSIFICATION SECTION AT THE END OF THE QUESTIONNAIRE.

*   *   *   *   *   *   *   *   *   *   *

12. How do you calculate the savings which can be accomplished by self-insuring risk rather than transferring it to a commercial insurance company? (Check as many boxes as are applicable.)

By comparing forecasted payments of losses and administrative costs against currently quoted premiums for commercial coverage	62.7%
By comparing actual payments of losses and administrative costs over a period of time against previously quoted insurance premiums for same period	62.7
By relying on calculations made by outside consultants or brokers	23.9
Other	8.5
No calculation of savings made	9.2

13. Are you able to get reliable quotes of commercial insurance premiums on the risk you are self-insuring?

Always	56.3%
Sometimes	32.9
Don't try	7.9
Seldom	2.9
	100.0%

14. Which of these means do you use to fund the losses you expect to incur in your self-insured risks? (Check as many boxes as are applicable.)

Separate bank accounts or securities	19.7%
Irrevocable trust funds with fiduciary	14.1
Payment of premiums to captive insurance company	14.1
Line of credit	12.0
Other funding methods	15.5
No funding	60.6

15. In order for your self-insurance program to be successful, do you consider it necessary to maintain complete and accurate records as to:

	Yes	No
Incidence of losses	97.1%	2.9%
Dollar magnitude of losses	97.9	2.1
Cost of handling and settling claims	81.6	18.4
Cost of loss prevention program	63.2	36.8
Cost of general administration of self-insurance program	72.3	27.7

16. In your internal accounting for self-insurance (other than with captive insurance company) do you:

	Yes	No
Charge expense accounts with amounts accrued for expected losses in advance of their known occurrence	33.8%	66.2%
Credit such loss accruals to an account carried as a liability on balance sheet	30.3	69.7
Credit such loss accruals to an account carried as reserve on balance sheet	25.2	74.8
Include forecasted self-insurance costs in operating budgets in same manner as commercial insurance costs	64.4	35.6
Segregate in-house administrative costs from the traditional accounts such as salaries, wages, supplies, etc. into accounts clearly labelled as a cost of self-insurance	12.5	87.5

17. When devising your self-insurance plan(s), which of the following were consulted? (Check as many boxes as are applicable.)

	Property	Liability	Workers' Compensation	Employee Benefits
Consulting firms	15.5%	14.8%	23.2%	28.9%
Insurance brokers	35.9	60.6	59.9	38.7
Insurance companies	24.6	25.4	28.9	31.7
Law firms	6.3	11.3	11.3	13.4
Accounting firms	4.2	5.6	4.2	5.6
Actuarial firms	2.1	1.4	3.5	19.0
Others	2.8	2.8	4.2	2.8
No outsiders consulted	15.5	9.2	12.0	7.7
We have no self-insurance plan for this coverage	20.4	21.8	14.1	21.8

18. If any outside consultants were involved in devising your plan(s), in what phases were the consultants involved? (Check as many boxes as are applicable.)

	Property	Liability	Workers' Compensation	Employee Benefits
Feasibility studies	21.1%	26.1%	31.7%	34.5%
Plan definition	7.0	11.3	18.3	22.5
Plan implementation	7.7	13.4	19.7	22.5
No outside consultants	31.7	26.8	24.6	21.8

19. Who handles claim settlements under your self-insurance plan(s)?

	Property	Liability	Workers' Compensation	Employee Benefits
In-house staff	37.3%	30.6%	24.0%	25.6%
Insurance company	16.1	21.5	20.8	39.2
Claim adjuster	11.9	14.0	21.6	3.2
Insurance broker	5.9	5.0	5.6	1.6
Other	1.7	4.9	8.8	4.8
We have no self-insurance plan for this coverage	27.1	24.0	19.2	25.6
	100.0%	100.0%	100.0%	100.0%

31

20. Who handles administration (other than claims) of your self-insurance plan(s)?

	Property	Liability	Workers' Compensation	Employee Benefits
In-house staff	57.6%	59.0%	51.2%	48.8%
Insurance company	6.8	4.9	11.2	17.3
Insurance broker	4.2	5.7	4.8	3.2
Administrative services firm	1.7	3.3	11.2	6.3
Other	.9	1.7	.8	-
We have no self-insurance plan for this coverage	28.8	25.4	20.8	24.4
	100.0%	100.0%	100.0%	100.0%

For classification purposes only

a) What is your principal business activity?

Manufacturing, processing	50.0%
Transportation, utilities	13.2
Wholesale-retail trade	14.6
Services	9.6
Banking, finance, real estate	8.6
Agriculture	1.5
Mining, minerals	1.5
Construction	1.0
	100.0%

b) Approximate annual revenues:

More than $1 billion	16.7%
$500 to $999 million	15.2
$250 to $499 million	15.7
$100 to $249 million	22.2
$25 to $99 million	21.7
Under $25 million	8.5
	100.0%

c) Approximate total assets:

More than $1 billion	22.7%
$500 to $999 million	10.6
$250 to $499 million	11.1
$100 to $249 million	17.7
$25 to $99 million	24.7
Under $25 million	13.2
	100.0%

d) Approximate number of employees:

More than 20,000	10.0%
10,000 to 19,999	9.6
5,000 to 9,999	15.2
2,000 to 4,999	27.3
500 to 1,999	27.3
Under 500	10.6
	100.0%

e) How many full-time professional personnel are engaged in risk/insurance management in your organization?

None	30.2%
1 - 10	65.6
More than 10	4.2
	100.0%

f) Title of person principally completing this questionnaire:

Risk/insurance manager	45.5%
Treasurer	22.5
Vice president - finance	12.9
Controller	10.7
President	5.1
Other	3.3
	100.0%

Chapter 5

What the Answers Mean

The purpose of this chapter is to analyze the responses to the 26 questions contained in the survey instrument. These responses were enumerated in "The Questions and the Answers."[1] The first 11 questions were directed to both those who self-insure and those who do not, followed by nine questions addressed only to self-insurers. The final group of six classification questions were to be completed by all respondents.

To aid the reader in comparing his firm with the firms in our study group, we analyze the classification questions first.[2] These questions cover type of industry, annual revenue, total assets, number of employees, number of full-time professional risk management personnel, and the title of the person completing the questionnaire.

One is never too old to learn from others—to borrow from a well-known adage. Nor is one likely to be too smart or sophisticated to learn from others. We had that fact brought home to us many times during the year or so we worked on this study. We sincerely hope that the reader, too, will be able to profit from learning what other similarly situated companies are doing about self-insurance.

Classification Section

The first question in the classification section asked respondents to name their principal business activity. Their responses were coded into nine broad categories as shown by Table 1 on page 36. When cross tabulated with a firm's status as a self-insurer, it is clear that its type of business is not likely to affect its decision to self-insure or not self-insure. Six industry groups are within five percentage points of the 71.7% overall figure for respondents self-

---

[1] The exact wording of the questions and the exact count of the responses were placed in a separate chapter in order to allow greater freedom in this chapter to emphasize the more important findings.

[2] While the discussion in this chapter does not follow the same order as the questionnaire, responses to all questions are discussed.

TABLE 1

Principal Business Activity

	Self-Insurers	Non-Self-Insurers
Agriculture	66.7%	33.3%
Mining and petroleum	66.7	33.3
Construction	0.0	100.0
Manufacturing	74.7	25.3
Communications, transportation and utilities	69.2	30.8
Wholesale trade	66.7	33.3
Retail trade	80.0	20.0
Finance and real estate	58.8	41.2
Services	73.7	26.3
All respondents	71.7	28.3

$X^2 = 7.89$ Significance = .4439[3]

insuring. Of the other three, construction is represented by only two companies—hardly a representative sample. The finance and real estate group is somewhat below the overall percentage, and the retail trade group is somewhat above the overall percentage.

Subjects also were asked to indicate which of six categories included their approximate annual revenue. (See Table 2.) Here we found a strong

TABLE 2

Annual Revenue

	Self-Insurers	Non-Self-Insurers
More than $1 billion	87.9%	12.1%
$500 to $999 million	90.0	10.0
$250 to $499 million	90.3	9.7
$100 to $249 million	65.9	34.1
$25 to $99 million	53.5	46.5
Under $25 million	35.3	64.7

$X^2 = 33.38$ Significance = .0001

---

[3] The null hypothesis is that there is no relationship between a company's line of business and its decision to self-insure or not self-insure. The X^2 test shows that there is a 44% probability of the null hypothesis occurring; this is too large a probability to permit rejection of the null hypothesis in Table 1. On the other hand, in Table 2, the Chi-square (X^2) test shows only a .01% probability that amount of annual revenue and the decision to self-insure are not positively related.

positive relationship between firms' self-insurance status and their annual revenue. Of the 63 firms having more than $500 million in annual revenue, 89% self-insure, while 48% of the firms having less than $100 million self-insure. The mean annual revenue is $531.0 million for all respondents, while it is $592 million for self-insurers and $379.2 million for non-self-insurers.[4]

The relationship between amount of assets and a firm's self-insuring status is similar to that of revenue. (See Table 3.) The correlation (Pearson's R) between revenue and assets, however, is .45, indicating a different distribution. Where 89% of firms having over $500 million in annual revenue self-insure, 81% of the firms having over $500 million in assets self-insure. Of firms having less than $100 million in assets, 55% self-insure in contrast to 48% of those whose annual revenue is less than $100 million. The mean amount of assets for all respondents is $1.0 billion, while the means for self-insurers and non-self-insurers are $1.2 billion and $504 million, respectively. The t-test for the difference between means for self-insurers and non-self-insurers indicates self-insurers have higher assets, with 98.3% confidence.

TABLE 3

Amount of Assets

	Self-Insurers	Non-Self-Insurers
More than $1 billion	77.8%	22.2%
$500 to $999 million	90.5	9.5
$250 to $499 million	86.4	13.6
$100 to $249 million	80.0	20.0
$25 to $99 million	61.2	38.8
Under $25 million	42.3	57.7

$X^2 = 21.72$ Significance = .0006

Another measure of relative size is number of employees. Separated by firms' self-insuring status, they fall into the six size ranges as shown in Table 4. The t-test of significance of difference between means establishes that self-insurers have higher number of employees, with 98% confidence. The mean number of employees for all respondents is 7,510, whereas the means for self-insurers and non-self-insurers are 8,790 and 4,450 respectively.

---

[4] Annual revenue, assets, net income, number of employees, and net income amounts were obtained for 190 of 198 respondents from a source independent of the questionnaire. Instead of using the broad categories reported in response to the questionnaire, we used the independent actual amounts in calculating means and differences between means.

TABLE 4

Number of Employees

	Self-Insurers	Non-Self-Insurers
More than 20,000	85.0%	15.0%
10,000 to 19,999	100.0	0.0[5]
5,000 to 9,999	90.0	10.0
2,000 to 4,999	75.9	24.1
500 to 1,999	53.7	46.3
Under 500	42.9	57.1

$X^2 = 31.91$ Significance = .0001

Not a part of the questionnaire, but nonetheless important, is the size of the net income of our respondents, which we obtained from an independent source. The mean net income for 190[6] respondents is $25.9 million. The mean net income for self-insurers and non-self-insurers, respectively, is $29.9 million and $16.0; such means follow approximately the same pattern as with revenues. Again, the t-test indicates the difference between means is significant at the 95% level of confidence.

In order to delve into the question of whether self-insurance decisions were affected by insurance department staffing, subjects were asked how many full-time risk management professionals were in their employ. Responses showed that 70% of the companies have one or more full-time persons (76% of the self-insurers vs. 52% of the non-self-insurers). Only 4% of the respondents have more than 10 full-time risk management professionals.[7]

Finally, we asked for the title of the person completing the questionnaire. (See Table 5.) For both self-insurers and non-self-insurers, the person most often completing the questionnaire was the risk/insurance manager. For non-self-insurers, however, the percentage of questionnaires completed by a risk/insurance manager is much lower, reflecting, no doubt, the absence of such a title in many smaller companies.

*   *   *   *   *

Now we shall proceed to elaborate on our perception of the significant meanings of respondents' answers to the two sections of the questionnaire that deal directly with the subject of self-insurance.

---

[5] The use of the Chi-square test is dependent on *expected* cell frequency, which is 5.4 in this case.

[6] Net income for eight companies was not shown in the independent source.

[7] In a TIME study in 1975, it was found that 4.6% of their respondents had nine or more professional personnel in their risk/insurance departments.

TABLE 5

Person Completing Questionnaire

	Self-Insurers	Non-Self-Insurers
President	0.8%	9.8%
Vice President, Finance	11.0	17.6
Treasurer	23.6	19.6
Risk/Insurance Manager	52.1	29.5
Controller	3.1	9.8
Other	9.4	13.7
	100.0%	100.0%

$X^2 = 18.15$ Significance = .0028

The Policy Decision

The first question asked of our sample firms is one of the most important questions facing active or prospective self-insurers—"Who will make self-insurance policy decisions?" When cross tabulated with the firms' self-insuring status, the results show that the person who makes policy decisions for the most part is the same for both those who self-insure and those who do not. (See Table 6.) Those differences which are evident might have been predicted. Policy decisions for self-insuring firms are more often made by the chief financial officer and less often by the chief executive. The reverse is true for those firms not self-insuring.

TABLE 6

Policy Decision Maker

	Self-Insurers	Non-Self-Insurers
Board of directors	7.1%	7.1%
Chief executive	22.1	33.9
Chief financial officer	34.3	26.8
Insurance manager, including joint decision with others	20.7	17.8
Other	11.4	10.7
No policy decision	4.4	3.7
	100.0%	100.0%

$X^2 = 3.11$ Significance = .683

While the position of the person making the self-insurance policy decision seems unrelated to the presence of self-insurance, it does appear to be related to the size measures of revenue, assets and number of employees. Industry classification cannot be shown to be significantly related to the locus of the self-insurance policy decision (no table shown).

The relationship between approximate annual revenue and the position of the person who makes the self-insurance policy decision can be established. Referring to Table 7 (a larger table collapsed to eliminate small cell frequencies[8]), it can be seen that self-insurance policy decisions are much more likely to be made higher in the organization chart in companies with lower annual revenue than in companies with higher annual revenue. A similar relationship exists between the policy decision and amount of assets (no table shown).

TABLE 7

Self-Insurance Policy Decision Maker
by Annual Revenue

	Over $500 Million	$100 to 499 Million	Under $100 Million
Board of directors	4.8%	4.1%	13.3%
Chief executive	12.9	31.1	31.7
Chief financial officer	30.6	39.1	25.0
Insurance manager, including joint decision with others	32.3	20.3	6.7
Other, including no policy decision	19.4	5.4	23.3
	100.0%	100.0%	100.0%

X^2 = 30.43   Significance = .0002

Unlike other size factors, the number of employees on the payroll of a particular firm does not show a similar relationship to the person who makes self-insurance policy decisions. In companies having higher assets and annual revenue, the policy decision is made most often by the risk/insurance manager, closely followed in frequency by the chief financial officer. But firms with the most employees more often have policy decisions regarding self-insurance handed down by the chief financial officer. (See Table 8.) Companies in the middle range are almost equally divided among chief executive, chief financial officer and risk/insurance manager.

---

[8] Chi-square tests are unreliable when more than 20% of the expected frequencies are smaller than five or when any expected frequency is smaller than one.

40

TABLE 8

**Self-Insurance Policy Maker
by Number of Employees**

	Over 10,000[9]	2,000-9,999	Under 2,000
Board of directors	2.6%	2.4%	14.7%
Chief executive	7.9	30.1	29.3
Chief financial officer	42.1	28.9	30.7
Insurance manager, including joint decision with others	23.7	30.2	6.7
Other, including no policy decision	23.7	8.4	18.6
	100.0%	100.0%	100.0%

$X^2 = 32.96$ Significance = .001

The Specific Decision

Specific self-insurance decisions made by the respondents are made most often by either a financial officer (not necessarily the chief financial officer) or the risk/insurance manager. Which of these two individuals makes the decision is related to the two size factors mentioned earlier—amount of assets and amount of annual revenue.

Firms having more assets and higher revenue more often vest specific self-insurance decisions in a risk/insurance manager. On the other hand, firms with fewer assets and lower revenue—many of whom do not designate anyone as risk/insurance manager—rely on a financial officer for the specific decision. (See Tables 9 and 10.)

TABLE 9

**Specific Self-Insurance Decision Maker
by Amount of Annual Revenue**

	Over $500 Million	$100 to 499 Million	Under $100 Million
Financial officer	27.9%	46.7%	63.3%
Insurance manager	63.9	40.0	23.3
Other	8.2	13.3	13.4
	100.0%	100.0%	100.0%

$X^2 = 20.71$ Significance = .0004

---

[9] Only 20% of the respondents fall into the largest "number of employees" category, whereas 32% and 33% fall into the largest "revenue" and "total asset" categories.

TABLE 10

Specific Self-Insurance Decision Maker
by Amount of Assets

	Over $500 Million	$100 to 499 Million	Under $100 Million
Financial officer	26.6%	40.4%	66.7%
Insurance manager	64.1	45.6	21.3
Other	9.3	14.0	12.0
	100.0%	100.0%	100.0%

$X^2 = 27.10$ Significance = .0001

Timing of Self-Insurance Decisions

The decision for or against self-insurance must be made at some particular time in each company. This time may vary from one firm to another and from one coverage to another. Respondents indicated that the decision most likely was to be made either when risks were first identified or when commercial insurance policies expired. There does not appear to be any significant relationship between the timing of the self-insurance decision and size of company except that smaller companies in our sample are slightly more likely to make a one-time decision that becomes standing policy. Differences in timing of the self-insurance decision between those who self-insure and those who do not are not statistically significant. (See Table 11.)

TABLE 11

Timing of Self-Insurance Decisions

	Self-Insurers	Non-Self-Insurers
When commercial policies expire	45.9%	34.5%
When risks are first identified	44.4	47.2
One-time decision	8.3	10.9
Other	1.4	7.4
	100.0%	100.0%

$X^2 = 5.60$ Significance = .1327

Factors Affecting the Decision

An important part of the study (perhaps *the* most important part) was to determine what considerations cause a firm to investigate self-insurance as an alternative to commercial insurance and influence its decision in favor of one or the other. Twelve factors thought likely to affect the decision were listed. Most of these factors can influence an enterprise against self-insurance as well as lead toward self-insurance, depending on a firm's particular circumstances.

Reference to the questionnaire (contained in Chapter 4) will show that respondents were asked to indicate the degree of importance of each of the 12 factors by checking "Heavy Influence," "Some Influence," or "No Influence." The distinction between "Heavy Influence" and "Some Influence" answers not always was sufficient to provide useful information for statistical analysis. In such instances, we reclassified the three choices into two, the result being "Some Influence" and "No Influence."

Financial Capacity to Withstand Losses

Our expectation that this factor would be the first and most important for those companies considering self-insurance was confirmed by the 99% who indicated that this factor influenced their self-insurance decisions. Cross tabulation with the presence of self-insurance, amount of annual revenue, amount of assets and number of employees indicated that the financial capacity to withstand losses is a crucial consideration regardless of size and regardless of whether the company decides to self-insure. For example, if the respondents are classified into three groups according to approximate annual revenue, 96.8% of the over $500 million group, 100% of the $100-$499 million group and 98.3% of the under $100 million group indicate they are influenced by financial capacity in making their decision for or against self-insurance.

Qualified Personnel to Administer Program

After financial capacity, availability of qualified personnel to administer the self-insurance program was the next most important consideration. Approximately 80% of the respondents indicated they were influenced by this factor.

Self-insurers in our sample were much more likely to be influenced by the availability of qualified personnel to administer the self-insurance program. (See Table 12.) They most often indicated "Some Influence" rather than "Heavy Influence." On the other hand, a substantially larger percentage of the non-self-insuring firms indicated they were not influenced at all. Put another way, it appears that the availability of qualified personnel has led to firms' entering into self-insurance practices.

Whether smaller companies tend to be less influenced by the availability of qualified personnel than larger companies depends upon which indicator of size you look at. When this factor is related to amount of annual revenue, companies with lower revenue much more often indicate "no influence." (See

TABLE 12

Influence of Availability of
Qualified Personnel

	Self-Insurers	Non-Self-Insurers
Heavy Influence	31.7%	23.5%
Some Influence	53.2	43.2
No Influence	15.1	. 33.3
	100.0%	100.0%

X^2 = 7.79   Significance = .0204

TABLE 13

Influence of Availability of Qualified
Personnel by Amount of
Annual Revenue

	Over $500 Million	$100 to 499 Million	Under $100 Million
Heavy Influence	31.7%	31.9%	23.6%
Some Influence	60.4	50.0	40.0
No Influence	7.9	18.1	36.4
	100.0%	100.0%	100.0%

X^2 = 15.38   Significance = .0040

Table 13.) But when this factor is related to amount of assets, the difference between companies with larger total assets and those with smaller total assets is not statistically significant (no table shown). The relationship between availability of qualified personnel and number of employees is similar to the relationship of the same factor to amount of revenue. Firms in our sample with a smaller number of employees most often indicated they were not influenced by the availability of qualified personnel.

Of the various industry groups in our sample, the group most likely to indicate that the availability of qualified personnel does not influence the self-insurance decision is the banking and real estate group. This group also shows the lowest correlation between annual revenue and amount of assets, R = .60, where the correlation for other industry classifications centers around R = .85. Were it not for this group of firms—which tend to have very large amounts of assets and small annual revenues—the relationship between influence of availability of qualified personnel to administer the self-insurance program and size of firm would be clear, and it could be established that smaller firms are less likely to be influenced by this factor.

Geographic or Similar Dispersion of Risks

According to Greene (1978), a dispersion of risks, so as to reduce or eliminate the possibility of a single loss assuming catastrophic proportions, is essential for self-insuring firms. We expected that most respondents would be influenced by this factor; approximately 70% of the respondents indicated that they were. There was no significant statistical relationship between the influence of geographic or similar dispersion of risks and any of the size or other variables, including the presence of self-insurance. Thus, this factor can be characterized as being important to a broad group of companies but not as broad a group as financial capacity or qualified personnel.

Emphasis on In-House Loss Prevention Program

Respondents were divided on this factor, with self-insurers being much more prone to indicate they were influenced by an emphasis on in-house loss prevention programs. (See Table 14.) When "Heavy Influence" and "Some Influence" are combined, 82.7% of the self-insurers and 55.8% of those not self-insuring indicated they were influenced.

TABLE 14

Influence of Emphasis on In-House
Loss Prevention

	Heavy	Some	None	Total
Self-Insurers	25.9%	56.8%	17.3%	100.0%
Non-Self-Insurers	25.0	30.8	44.2	100.0

$X^2 = 16.32$ Significance = .0003

None of the size variables was significantly related to the influence of emphasis on in-house loss prevention program, but industry classification of our respondents does appear to relate to this factor. (See Table 15.) Manufacturing, transportation and utility firms were most influenced, with real estate, banking and services being least influenced. The group most often indicating "Heavy Influence" was the wholesale/retail trade group.

Nonavailability of Commercial Insurance

Due to the recent tight market in product liability insurance, we expected many firms to be forced into self-insurance programs because commercial insurance would be unavailable. Approximately one-third of the respondents indicated they were influenced by this factor. Relationships between both size and industry classification and influence of nonavailability of commercial insurance can be seen. (See Tables 16 and 17.)

TABLE 15

Influence of Emphasis on In-House Loss Prevention by Industry

	Some	None
Manufacturing	81.2%	18.8%
Transportation, utilities	88.5	11.5
Wholesale/retail trade	69.0	31.0
Finance and real estate	62.5	37.5
Others	54.2	45.8

$X^2 = 12.08$ Significance = .0168

TABLE 16

Influence of Nonavailability of Commercial Insurance by Firms' Assets

	Some	None
Over $500 million	44.6%	55.4%
$100 to $499 million	27.3	72.7
Under $100 million	28.2	71.8

$X^2 = 12.71$ Significance = .0100

TABLE 17

Influence of Nonavailability of Commercial Insurance by Industry

	Some	None
Manufacturing	32.3%	67.7%
Transportation, utilities	56.0	44.0
Wholesale/retail trade	10.7	89.3
Finance and real estate	43.8	56.3
Others	34.6	65.4

$X^2 = 13.08$ Significance = .0111

Dividing subjects into three groups based on amount of assets, those firms in the group with the largest assets were the most likely to indicate they were influenced by nonavailability of commercial insurance. When relating this factor to industry classification, it can be seen that transportation and utility firms most often are influenced. We assume that commercial airliners and nuclear power plants heavily influence these statistics.

Nonaffordability of Commercial Insurance

We expected responses as to the influence of this factor on the self-insurance decision to differ between self-insurers and non-self-insurers and also between industry classifications. We expected smaller companies to be more influenced than larger. We were only partially correct.

Differences between the responses to this question of those self-insuring and those not self-insuring are not statistically significant. The percentage of self-insurers responding "Heavy Influence," however, is double that of non-self-insurers—supporting the notion that nonaffordability of commercial insurance provides some impetus for self-insuring.

When inability to afford commercial insurance is cross tabulated with industry classification, one can see that some industries are much more influenced than others. (See Table 18.) Manufacturers tend to be most

TABLE 18

Influence of Nonaffordability of Commercial Insurance by Industry

	Heavy	Some	None	Total
Manufacturing	21.6%	34.1%	44.3%	100.0%
Transportation, utilities	8.0	44.0	48.0	100.0
Wholesale/retail trade	3.6	25.0	71.4	100.0
Finance and real estate	6.3	18.8	74.9	100.0
Others	4.0	36.0	60.0	100.0

X^2 = 17.51   Significance = .0252

heavily influenced. For manufacturers, the incidence of citing "Heavy Influence" is almost three times greater than for the next most frequent group. If those responding "Heavy Influence" and "Some Influence" are combined into one group, transportation and utility firms closely follow manufacturers in indicating that inability to afford commercial insurance influenced the self-insurance decision.

The relationship of size of firm based on amount of assets, annual revenue, and number of employees to this factor cannot be established statistically. However, 59% of firms with less than $100 million in annual revenue and 55% of those firms with less than $100 million in assets indicated that inability to afford commercial insurance is a factor in their self-insurance decisions. These percentages are somewhat higher than the percentage of larger firms, indicating that smaller firms may be more greatly influenced by this factor.

Before leaving the "nonaffordability" subject, we should mention that we sensed some uncertainty on the part of some respondents as to the meaning of the term. Some apparently took it to mean "available only at an excessive price." There is considerable sympathy for such meaning—it just doesn't happen to be the one intended in the questionnaire.

Loading (Profit) Included in Commercial Insurance Premiums

An obvious method for increasing profits is to cut costs. Choosing self-insurance over commercial insurance with the objective of reducing insurance expense by the amount of the insurer's profit is a cost-cutting measure and is a factor in the self-insurance decision of the respondent firms in our study.

We expected self-insurers to be much more conscious of insurance company profits when considering self-insurance. The study shows that loading on commercial insurance policies is five times more likely to "heavily" influence the decisions of self-insurers than non-self-insurers. The percentage of self-insurers indicating either "Heavy Influence" or "Some Influence" was 60%, whereas the percentage of firms not self-insuring who indicated they are influenced was 43%. (X^2 significance = .01)

Industry classification apparently is related to the influence of loading on commercial policies on the self-insurance decision for our sample firms. (See Table 19.) Companies most influenced are manufacturers. They were most likely to indicate "Heavy Influence" and also most likely to indicate

TABLE 19

Influence of Loading on Commercial Policies by Industry

	Some	None
Manufacturing	67.4%	32.6%
Transportation, utilities	42.3	57.7
Wholesale/retail trade	57.1	42.9
Finance and real estate	37.5	62.5
Others	36.0	64.0

$X^2 = 13.24$ Significance = .0102

"Some Influence." The group indicating they were least affected was the real estate, banking and services group. With regard to size of firm, larger firms (more than $500 million in annual revenue) more often indicated they were influenced by insurance company profits than did smaller firms.

(During the course of a conversation with an official of one of the respondents, we were informed that at least one insurance company had

48

suddenly decided it could reduce its rates when faced with the prospect of losing out to a self-insurance plan.)

Tying-Up Funds in Commercial Premiums and/or Deposits

Various commercial insurance plans require rather large advance premium payments or deposits even though a substantial portion of the advance payment or deposit may be refunded at some later date. When devising the questionnaire, we expected some firms to consider self-insurance in anticipation of being able to use such funds to such sufficient advantage that they would realize savings over commercial insurance. Self-insuring firms should, therefore, be influenced more heavily by this factor than those not self-insuring. We found this to be the case. (See Table 20.) Of those respondent firms mentioning "Heavy Influence," the ratio of self-insurers to non-self-insurers is more than 3:1.

TABLE 20

Influence of Tying-Up Funds in Commercial Insurance

	Heavy	Some	None
Self-Insurers	32.6%	40.6%	26.8%
Non-Self-Insurers	9.6	50.4	40.0

$X^2 = 10.64$ Significance = .0049

Insurance companies have devised ways of reducing "up front" payments in order to combat the tendency of firms to turn to self-insurance. An example is subtracting an estimated retrospective credit from the annual premium before calculating the monthly payment—a prospective retrospective adjustment, if we may join those contradictory terms. Another example, which is becoming more prevalent, is reducing the deposit to, say, 25% of its former amount, basing premium payments on monthly reported amounts of payrolls, inventories, and such, and applying the deposit to the premiums of the last two or three months of the policy year. While these examples were not included in our questionnaire, we believe that they, so-called "cash flow retro plans," and other cash flow enhancement measures by insurance companies have reduced the number of firms that are influenced toward self-insurance by large deposits and advance premiums.

Predisposition of Chief or Other Top Executives

Clearly, if the chief executive were strongly disposed toward self-insurance, many firms would be more likely to self-insure. The reverse also should be true. On the other hand, in a firm whose chief executive tends to leave such matters to others without interfering, the predisposition toward or away from self-insuring would not be significant. We found 41.6% of our respondents are influenced by the predisposition of a chief or top executive toward or away from self-insurance. We could not find significant relationships between this factor and size of firm or decision to self-insure or not self-insure.

Nondeductibility for Tax Purposes of Self-Insurance Accruals

On the surface, at least, it seems reasonable to assume that many firms would choose commercial insurance over self-insurance because self-insurance accruals are not deductible from income for federal income taxes. We expected firms not self-insuring to be more influenced by this factor than self-insuring firms. Our expectation was borne out in that we found 54.7% of the firms not self-insuring indicating their self-insurance decisions are influenced by nondeductibility for income taxes versus 41.3% of self-insuring firms (X^2 = 3.5969, significance = .057). There were no significant relationships between this factor and any of the size variables based on revenues, assets or employees.

Financial Accounting Standards Board Prohibition of Self-Insurance Accruals

Goshay's study published in 1978 by the Financial Accounting Standards Board (see "Other Studies") was summarized by the remark, "Based on the findings, the author concludes that Statement No. 5 did not affect the way firms made risk and insurance management decisions." Because this report was made available while our questionnaire was being formulated, we decided not to delve into this matter in any depth. In order for the "influence" section of the questionnaire to be complete, however, we did ask our firms the extent to which their self-insurance decision was influenced by the prohibition of accruals in their accounts. Whereas Goshay's study was designed to test only this one question, our study made only one reference to FASB No. 5. We expected our respondents to overwhelmingly indicate they are not influenced by this factor in light of Goshay's finding. To the contrary, 37.8% indicated they *are* influenced by FASB Statement No. 5 in their self-insurance decisions, although only 6.9% indicated "Heavy Influence." The percentage, as expected, was higher for those not self-insuring, but only slightly. The percentage of firms having more than $500 million in assets indicating they are influenced was higher—45%—than for smaller firms. It seems unlikely that FASB No. 5 would be influencing these large firms, 89% of whom are self-insurers, toward self-insurance. Therefore, if the self-insurance decisions of these firms are influenced by this factor, it must be toward not self-insuring certain risks they otherwise might have self-insured.

Risk Management Methods

To this point in this chapter, we have discussed various aspects of the self-insurance decision including who makes it, when it is made, and the factors influencing the decision. We come now to more specific information about how decisions are made.

The subject firms were asked *how risks were identified.* (See Table 21.) For this question multiple responses were permitted where a firm used some combination of the methods listed. Property risk identification is derived most often from a balance sheet analysis, internally developed check lists, analysis by outside broker, consultant or insurance company, or a combination of these methods. Liability risks are identified most often by use of

TABLE 21

How Risks Are Identified

	Property	Liability	Workers' Compensation	Employee Benefits
Balance sheet analysis	54.5%	28.8%	15.2%	12.1%
Check list—developed internally	52.0	51.0	46.5	43.4
Check list—developed externally	18.2	17.2	15.7	13.1
Analysis by outside broker, consultant or insurance company	54.0	56.1	53.0	54.5
Other	13.1	14.6	13.6	10.1

internally developed check lists and analysis by outsiders. As expected, the balance sheet isn't of as much use with the liability risk because it would relate to a *contingent* liability, which may or may not appear in the balance sheet or accompanying footnotes.

The use of internally generated check lists was much more prevalent in larger companies, except for employee benefits. (See Table 22.) We expected smaller companies to make greater use of outside help in risk identification, and such pattern is evident in Table 23. The lesser use of outsiders by the grouping of smallest companies probably results from some of them not really attempting to identify their risks.

Techniques for estimating the dollar magnitude of risks vary widely. (See Table 24.) As a whole, our subjects most often indicated they relied on informal judgments to estimate the dollar magnitude of risks (36.4%), followed by loss probability studies performed internally. Self-insurers in the study group were three times as likely to indicate loss probability studies performed internally as those firms not self-insuring. Non-self-insurers rely

TABLE 22

**Use of Internally Developed Check Lists
by Annual Revenue**

	Over $500 Million	$100 to 499 Million	Under $100 Million
Property	61.9%	58.7%	33.3%
Liability	61.9	52.0	38.3
Workers' Compensation	57.1	49.3	31.7
Employee Benefits	44.4	44.0	41.7

TABLE 23

**Use of Outside Broker, Consultant
or Insurance Company
by Annual Revenue**

	Over $500 Million	$100 to 499 Million	Under $100 Million
Property	39.7%	64.0%	56.7%
Liability	38.1	68.0	60.0
Workers' Compensation	36.5	65.3	55.0
Employee Benefits	42.9	69.3	48.3

TABLE 24

Methods for Estimating Dollar Magnitude of Risks

	Self-Insurers	Non-Self-Insurers
Loss probability study performed internally	27.9%	7.3%
Loss probability study performed by outside consultant, broker or insurance company	12.1	12.7
Asset amounts shown on balance sheet	3.6	9.1
Informal determination based on judgment and experience	33.6	43.6
Other	.7	1.8
Various combinations of the above	22.1	25.5
	100.0%	100.0%

$X^2 = 11.70$ Significance = .0391

much more heavily on informal judgment than do self-insurers. These differences are statistically significant based on a Chi-square test.

Few business decisions are irrevocable. Perhaps insurance decisions tend to be more temporary than some others because insurance programs may be modified, adding coverage, increasing deductibles or self-insuring as the position of the firm and the nature of its risks change over time or as attitudes of the firm's executives change. Add to this the variability of the insurance market, and changes in insurance practices seem almost certain for all but the smallest firms.

Our subjects were asked *how often self-insurance decisions are re-evaluated.* Almost half the respondents indicated their property self-insurance decisions are re-evaluated annually (45.9%); the next most frequently mentioned timing for re-evaluation was "As Changes Dictate." (See Table 25.) Differences between firms self-insuring and those not self-insuring are not statistically significant with regard to the frequency with which property self-insurance decisions are re-evaluated.

TABLE 25

Frequency of Re-Evaluation of Self-Insurance Decision

	Annually	Within 2-5 Years	As Circumstances Change	Not Consciously Done	Total
Property	45.4%	14.4%	34.5%	5.7%	100.0%
Liability	49.2	9.4	35.2	6.2	100.0
Workers' compensation	45.3	13.0	33.4	8.3	100.0
Employee benefits	38.2	11.0	41.9	8.9	100.0

Self-insurance decisions for liability risks are re-evaluated with much the same frequency as property risks. Again, there is no significant difference in timing between self-insurers and non-self-insurers. Most of the respondents indicated that the workers' compensation decision is re-evaluated annually, but self-insuring firms and firms not self-insuring differ significantly on this point. (See Table 26.) Self-insurers re-evaluate workers' compensation risks annually most often. Firms not self-insuring indicated these risks more often are re-evaluated as changes dictate.

As well as current self-insurance practices and decisions, respondents were asked about the *future of self-insurance.* Specifically, they were asked whether they were more likely to increase, decrease or leave unchanged their self-insurance during the next five years.

Of the self-insurers, 64% indicated they would increase self-insurance for property risks during the next five years. This figure contrasts with 46% of

TABLE 26

Frequency of Re-Evaluation of Workers' Compensation Decision

	Annually	Within 2-5 Years	As Circumstances Change	Not Consciously Done	Total
Self-insurers	49.6%	14.9%	29.1%	6.4%	100.0%
Non-self-insurers	35.8	7.5	43.5	13.2	100.0

$X^2 = 7.78$ Significance = .0507

the firms not self-insuring. Larger firms are significantly more likely to increase self-insurance for property risks than smaller firms. Such likelihood was found in 74.2% of firms with over $500 million in assets, 55.4% of firms with $100 to $499 million in assets, and 48.6% of firms with less than $100 million in assets.

The pattern of responses with regard to future plans for self-insuring liability, workers' compensation and employee benefits insurance risks is quite similar to that for property insurance risks. Approximately 60% of self-insuring firms will increase their self-insured exposure during the next five years. A lesser percentage (approximately 44%) of firms not self-insuring are likely to increase their self-insurance. Combined, approximately 55% of our respondents expect to increase their self-insurance coverage, which is quite similar to a 52% expectation found by *Fortune* in 1973. (See "Other Studies.")

*   *   *   *

We have discussed the answers to all the questions in the first section of the questionnaire except for questions 4, 5 and 6 dealing with respondents' degree of involvement in self-insurance. We have set aside a separate chapter—"Who Self-Insures the Most?"—for an in-depth look at this involvement and will offer only a few general findings here.

Large deductibles (more than 10% of risk) were used most frequently to self-insure property and liability risks. Formal *self-insurance programs* were used most frequently for workers' compensation and employee benefit coverages. (Interestingly, the single largest incidence of self-insurance shown by the responses to question 4 is that 36.4% of the businesses have a self-insurance plan for workers' compensation.) *Captive insurance companies* are used sparingly but rather consistently among all types of risks except employee benefits, where only one of the respondents uses a captive. We counted the number of companies checking at least one risk category under each of the risk handling methods shown in question 4, and the results are shown at the top of the next page.

Total companies	198
Commercial insurance	195
Large deductibles	83
Self-insurance program	121
Captive insurance company	24
No insurance	54[10]

Question 5 responses were used to develop the Self-Insurance Index used in the separate chapter mentioned previously.

We asked our respondents in question 6 to estimate what percentage of their total self-insured risk (for all types of exposures combined) is being handled by the various self-insurance techniques. Their responses were averaged, with the following results:

Large deductibles	31%
Self-insurance program	53
Captive insurance company	6
No insurance	10
	100%

Management of Self-Insurance

We now turn to a discussion of the answers to those questions directed only to the 142 self-insurers. The focus thus far has been the self-insurance decision—how, when and by whom it is made and the factors influencing the decision. The remainder of this chapter covers self-insurers and the management of their self-insurance practices. The discussion is divided into three sections headed Planning and Implementation, Administration, and Accounting.

Planning and Implementation

We asked subjects for specific details regarding the type of help sought from outsiders during the planning stage of their self-insurance programs. (See Table 27.) We listed several typical sources of outside help and gave the respondent space to list others.

The most prevalent source of help for all risks is insurance brokers, followed by insurance companies. For property insurance, subjects consulted insurance brokers (50%), insurance companies (24.6%) and consulting firms (15.5%). For liability risks, the pattern is very similar, except for these

---

[10] A visual scan of answers in the "no insurance" column reveals that many companies checked this column when the risk was not present—e.g., a bank with no inventories. The questionnaire was faulty in not providing a "risk not present" column.

TABLE 27

Firms Consulted in Planning
Self-Insurance

	Property	Liability	Workers' Compensation	Employee Benefits
Consulting firms	15.5%	14.8%	23.2%	28.9%
Insurance brokers	50.0	60.6	59.9	38.7
Insurance companies	24.6	25.4	28.9	31.7
Law firms	6.3	11.3	11.3	13.4
Accounting firms	4.2	5.6	4.2	5.6
Actuarial firms	2.1	1.4	3.5	19.0
Others	2.8	2.8	4.2	2.8
No outsiders consulted	15.5	9.2	12.0	7.7
We have no self-insurance plan for this coverage	20.4	21.8	14.1	21.8

risks law firms were consulted twice as often as for property risks, which is not unexpected.

For workers' compensation plans and employee benefits programs, insurance brokers and insurance companies again were consulted, but the percentage of firms conferring with consulting firms for this type of coverage is much higher than for property and liability risks. Actuarial firms were consulted by 19% of the respondents with regard to employee benefits plans, and law firms were consulted by 13.4%.

Planning aid was sought most often for feasibility studies. (See Table 28.) In this phase, 34.5% of the subjects used outside help for employee benefits programs and 31.7% for workers' compensation. The percentage seeking assistance with feasibility studies on self-insurance for property and liability risks was smaller but still substantial.

TABLE 28

Phase of Planning in Which
Consultants Were Involved

	Property	Liability	Workers' Compensation	Employee Benefits
Feasibility studies	21.1%	26.1%	31.7%	34.5%
Plan definition	7.0	11.3	18.3	22.5
Plan implementation	7.7	13.4	19.7	22.5
No outside consultants	31.7	26.8	24.6	21.8

Use of outside consultants for plan definition and plan implementation was most prevalent for workers' compensation and employee benefits.

Administration of Self-Insurance

The administrative burden of self-insurance can be overwhelming because a self-insuring firm has to arrange for services once provided by a commerical insurer. These services include claims handling, claims settlement and accounting, among others.

Claim adjusting and settlement most often are handled by in-house staff. (See Table 29.) Patterns are very similar for property and liability risks, but for employee benefits the percentage of firms using insurance companies is much larger. Claims adjusters are hired for workers' compensation claims more often than for other risks.

TABLE 29

Source of Claim Settlement Services

	Property	Liability	Workers' Compensation	Employee Benefits
In-house staff	37.4%	30.6%	24.0%	25.6%
Insurance company	16.1	21.5	20.8	39.2
Insurance broker	5.9	5.0	5.6	1.6
Claim adjusters	11.9	14.0	21.6	3.2
Others	1.6	4.9	8.8	4.8
No self-insurance for this coverage	27.1	24.0	19.2	25.6
	100.0%	100.0%	100.0%	100.0%

Administration other than claims settlement also is usually handled by in-house staffs of respondent firms. For workers' compensation and employee benefits plans, an insurance company is used more often than for property and liability risks. With the exception of workers' compensation plans, administrative services firms are rarely used by our respondents. (See Table 30.)

Accounting for Self-Insurance

An important aspect of every self-insurance plan is evaluating it in terms of its cost against the cost of commerical insurance for the same coverage. We asked respondents how savings from self-insuring are calculated. (See Table 31.) They compare both forecasted and actual costs of administration and

TABLE 30

Source of Administrative Services

	Property	Liability	Workers' Compensation	Employee Benefits
In-house staff	57.7%	59.1%	51.2%	48.9%
Insurance company	6.8	4.9	11.2	17.3
Insurance broker	4.2	5.7	4.8	3.1
Administrative services firm	1.7	3.3	11.2	6.3
Others	.8	1.6	.8	0.0
We have no plan for this coverage	28.8	25.4	20.8	24.4
	100.0%	100.0%	100.0%	100.0%

TABLE 31

Method of Calculating Savings

	% Yes Answers
By comparing forecasted payments of losses and administrative costs against currently quoted premiums for commercial coverage	62.7%
By comparing actual payments of losses and administrative costs over a period of time against previously quoted insurance premiums for same period	62.7
By relying on calculations made by outside consultants or brokers	23.9
Other	8.5
No calculation of savings made	9.2

losses with quoted commercial insurance premiums in most cases. Approximately 24% of the companies rely on outside brokers or consultants to calculate the amount of savings achieved for at least one self-insurance plan.

If savings on self-insurance plans are calculated by comparing them with quoted insurance premiums for the same risks, the reliability of such quotations is extremely important. Subjects were asked if they were able to get reliable quotes of commercial premiums on self-insured risks. Most firms feel they do get reliable quotes (56.4%) although the percentage is not overwhelming. A few firms don't try (7.9%), and the remainder indicated they sometimes (32.9%) or seldom (2.9%) get reliable quotes.

While technically not an accounting matter, an important question with regard to self-assumed risk is the funding of the risk or the use of other methods to protect the firm against sudden call on its working capital. Most of the respondents (60.6%) indicated they have no funding arrangement— implying they must feel sufficiently protected by current assets. Other firms use separate bank accounts or securities (19.7%), irrevocable trust funds (14.1%), premiums to a captive insurance company (14.1%), a line of credit (12.0%), or a combination of such funding methods. Hogue and Olson, in their 1976 study, found that 61% of the businesses that indicated it was not necessary for them to develop reserves to handle potential uninsured losses gave the reason that they absorb them from working capital. Although "reserving" is not always equivalent to "funding," it is interesting that our study and theirs found that 61% rely on working capital to absorb losses.

Determining the efficacy of a self-insurance plan requires record keeping. When asked what records are kept, our subjects responded that they record incidence of losses (97.1%), dollar magnitude of losses (97.9%), cost of handling and settling claims (81.6%), cost of loss prevention (63.2%), and the cost of general administration (72.3%).

Specifics of accounting as well as record keeping were also requested. Forecasted self-insurance costs are included in budgets in a manner similar to commercial insurance premiums by 64.4% of the companies. Self-insurance costs such as salaries, wages, supplies and other costs of administration are segregated in separate accounts by 12.5% of the respondents.

In light of the FASB Statement No. 5 prohibition, we were extremely surprised to learn that 33.8% of the respondents charge expense accounts with accruals for expected losses in advance of their known occurrence. One explanation may be that these accruals are reversed for annual financial statement purposes after use for internal reporting on a monthly basis during the year. Another possible explanation of the apparent flouting of the FASB prohibition against self-insurance charges in the income statement is that the sizes of such charges are considered immaterial. (The materiality principle, in effect, permits firms to violate other accounting principles if the amount involved isn't large enough to distort the finanical statements.)

Self-insurance accruals are credited to liability accounts in 30.3% of our respondents' balance sheets and to reserves in 25.2% of the cases. The combined total of 55.5% should have equalled the 33.8% of expense charges discussed in the preceding paragraph. The apparent discrepancy results from some companies' indicating that they use *both* liability and reserve accounts and from some companies' including in such liability and reserve accounts amounts pertaining to losses which have occurred but have not been settled. (This latter practice is not prohibited by FASB Statement No. 5, which relates only to making expense accruals for contingencies.)

Chapter 6

Who Self-Insures the Most?

The relationship between the relative size of a firm and its policy on self-insurance has been well-established in an earlier chapter. All indications are that the firms with larger revenue, assets, net income and number of employees are self-insurers more often than smaller firms. Where the earlier discussion establishes the existence of the relationship, the strength of the relationship remains to be described.

A reasonable hypothesis is that larger firms would tend to self-insure *more* than smaller firms. In the next few pages we will describe our attempt to test this hypothesis, as well as other relationships.

Self-insurance activity for any given firm can be limited to a single large deductible on a commercial policy requiring no self-insurance program at all. A firm also can assume 100% of the risk in several exposure areas, requiring professional risk management personnel to manage a self-insurance program that may include in-house administration of claims, loss control, and the like. Given the potential for diversity from one enterprise to another in self-insurance involvement, one may wonder whether there are significant and interesting relationships between relative level of self-insurance activity and any of the size or other characteristics described in other chapters. If such relationships can be established, and if the reader's firm fits into a particular pattern of characteristics, he or she will be able to compare his or her firm's involvement in self-insurance with that of other companies similarly situated.

A Self-Insurance Index

One way to compare a company's self-insurance involvement with that of another is to construct an index which can be used to quantify information regarding the firms' respective degrees of involvement in self-insurance. This index then can be calculated for all firms in the study and cross tabulated with other variables to give a profile of self-insurers.

Using the information provided by the respondents in the questionnaire, we devised self-insurance indexes measuring relative involvement in self-insurance in four areas—(1) overall, (2) property risks, (3) liability risks, and (4) workers' compensation and employee benefit risks. The construction of the indexes is arbitrary but, we believe, logical.

In question 5, respondents were asked to indicate how many of 14 different risks are self-insured. (See "The Questions and the Answers.") The risks are:

Property
    Buildings
    Machinery and equipment
    Inventories
    Business interruption
    Other property risks

Liability
    General (premises and operations)
    Products
    Auto
    Other liability risks

Workers' Compensation and Employee Benefits
    Workers' Compensation
    Employee Benefits
        Basic health
        Major medical
        Life
        Disability

We asked subjects to choose from five levels of involvement in self-insurance: None, 1% to 25%, 26% to 50%, 51% to 99%, and 100% of the various risks. We assigned progressive values to the groups, ranging from "O" for no self-insurance to "4" for 100% self-insurance of an exposure. If a firm self-insured 100% of every risk listed, a score of 56 would be obtained on the overall self-insurance index. Table 32 summarizes the possible scores and the actual scores in each risk area. By classification, non-self-insurers were excluded from all indexes even though they may have scored a few points from small deductibles on commercial policies.

The Validity of the Indexes

Having constructed the indexes as described, we tested their ability to aid in comparing the self-insurance program of one firm to that of another. If there are any significant relationships between the self-insurance indexes and size of firm, as measured by the attributes we have described elsewhere, these relationships should be consistent. For example, if the overall self-insurance

TABLE 32

The Self-Insurance Indexes

Risk Area	Maximum Possible Score	Maximum Actual Score	Mean Score	Median Score
Overall	56	39	15.72	14.33
Property	20	20	5.06	4.18
Liability	16	16	5.63	4.72
Workers' Compensation and Employee Benefits	20	16	5.03	4.31

index is related to assets, and we find evidence that firms with greater assets tend to score higher on the index, we should expect to find a similar relationship between the overall index and amounts of revenue or number of employees.

The median test[1] was performed for each of the four measures of size—revenue, assets, number of employees and net income—with each of the four self-insurance indexes to help establish the validity of the indexes. The test showed that a firm with an overall self-insurance index score above the median is likely to be above the median on all of the four size measures with 99.99% confidence. The same consistency exists for the liability risk index.

The property risk index showed a strong relationship to revenue and assets but a weaker relationship to number of employees and net income. The workers' compensation and employee benefits self-insurance index did not follow the other indexes in that it tended not to vary with the various size measures.

The Indexes Related to Size

The relationship between annual revenue and overall involvement in self-insurance is a strong one. Firms with more than $500 million in annual revenue are twice as likely to score above the median of 14.33 on the overall self-insurance index. (See Table 33.)

When related to firms' total assets, the property self-insurance index shows those with total assets over $500 million also having higher scores on this index. (See Table 34.) The table shows almost identical patterns for the medium-size companies and the smaller companies. Of the 142 self-insuring firms, 90.8% have some degree of self-insurance for property risks.

---

[1] For an explanation of the median test, see Siegel, *Nonparametric Statistics for the Behavioral Sciences,* McGraw-Hill, 1956, p. 111.

TABLE 33

Overall Self-Insurance Index

	Annual Revenue			
	Over $500 Million	$100 to 499 Million	Under $100 Million	All Companies
Scores over 14	71.4%	38.6%	27.6%	49.3%
Scores of 14 or less	28.6	61.4	72.4	50.7
	100.0%	100.0%	100.0%	100.0%

$X^2 = 19.05$ Significance = .00001

TABLE 34

Property Self-Insurance Index

	Amount of Assets			
	Over $500 Million	$100 to 499 Million	Under $100 Million	All Companies[2]
Scores over 4	63.0%	23.4%	19.5%	37.3%
Scores of 4 or less	37.0	76.6	80.5	62.7
	100.0%	100.0%	100.0%	100.0%

$X^2 = 24.63$ Significance = .0001

On the liability self-insurance index, as on the property index, larger firms score higher. (See Table 35.) Scores on this index generally tend to be somewhat higher, indicating that liability risks are self-insured to a greater degree than property risks.

TABLE 35

Liability Self-Insurance Index

	Annual Revenue			
	Over $500 Million	$100 to 499 Million	Under $100 Million	All Companies
Scores over 4	67.9%	45.6%	31.0%	51.4%
Scores of 4 or less	32.1	54.4	69.0	48.6
	100.0%	100.0%	100.0%	100.0%

$X^2 = 11.65$ Significance = .003

---

[2]Reference is made to the footnote to Table 39.

The other size measure to be related to the self-insurance indexes is approximate number of employees. The evidence indicates that the number of employees has less of an impact on involvement in self-insurance. The relationship is weaker than all of the previously described relationships between size of firm and the self-insurance indexes but still follows the general pattern of heavier self-insurance involvement by larger firms. (See Table 36.)

TABLE 36

Overall Self-Insurance Index

	Number of Employees			
	Over 10,000	2,000 to 9,999	Under 2,000	All Companies
Scores over 14	72.2%	47.1%	31.6%	49.3%
Scores of 14 or less	27.8	52.9	68.4	50.7
	100.0%	100.0%	100.0%	100.0%

$X^2 = 12.48$ Significance = .002

TABLE 37

**Workers' Compensation and Employee Benefits
Self-Insurance Index**

	Number of Employees			
	Over 10,000	2,000 to 9,999	Under 2,000	All Companies
Scores over 4	50.0%	47.1%	47.4%	47.9%
Scores of 4 or less	50.0	52.9	52.6	52.1
	100.0%	100.0%	100.0%	100.0%

$X^2 = 0.087$ Significance = .958

Because we found the property self-insurance index to be strongly related to asset totals and the liability index to revenues, we expected the workers' compensation and employee benefits index to be strongly related to number of employees. Such is not the case, however. (See Table 37.) Size, by the measure of number of employees, appears to have no bearing on a firm's self-insuring its "people" risks. A related conclusion is that small firms' self-insurance is highly concentrated in workers' compensation and employee benefits. (Their high score on this index and relatively low score on the overall index would necessitate low scores on the property and liability indexes.)

To summarize, we have described indexes of self-insurance involvement and have related them to various measures of size of firm. Size of firm was found to be strongly related to all of the self-insurance indexes except one, with larger firms having higher scores. Size of firm measured by number of employees was not related to the workers' compensation and employee benefits index.

The Indexes Related to Industry

In addition to the question of size, we were curious as to whether certain industries tend to get more deeply involved in self-insurance than other industries. In Table 38, respondents' industries have been divided into four

TABLE 38

Overall Self-Insurance Index

	Industry Group				
	Manufac- turing	Transportation/ Utilities	Wholesale/ Retail Trade	Others	All Companies
Over 28	5.4%	22.2%	4.5%	3.6%	7.1%
22 to 28	21.6	27.8	4.5	17.9	19.0
15 to 21	25.7	27.8	27.3	10.7	23.2
8 to 14	32.4	11.1	54.6	46.4	35.9
1 to 7	14.9	11.1	9.1	21.4	14.8
	100.0%	100.0%	100.0%	100.0%	100.0%

$X^2 = 87.71$ Significance = .00001

groups, and their self-insurance indexes have been tabulated in five "order of magnitude" groups. The table reveals that the heaviest self-insurers (those scoring above 14) are in the transportation/utility group, closely followed by the manufacturing group. The contrast between industry groups is even more pronounced at the "over 21" level. Only 9% of wholesale and retail firms were this deeply involved in self-insurance compared to 50% of the transportation and utility firms and 27% of the manufacturing firms.

When scores are divided into two groups at the median of 4.18, the property risk index also shows a significant relationship to type of industry. (See Table 39.) Firms in the transportation/utility group are more than twice as likely to score in excess of the median on the property self-insurance index than all firms combined. A cross tabulation of the liability self-insurance index along similar lines shows different but still similar relationships. (See Table 40.) The firms in the transportation/utility group are much more likely to score above the median, but the disparity between their scores and the other industry groups is not as great as in the property index.

TABLE 39

Property Self-Insurance Index

		Industry Group			
	Manufac-turing	Transportation/Utilities	Wholesale/Retail Trade	Others	All Companies[3]
Scores over 4	32.4%	77.8%	31.8%	28.6%	37.3%
Scores of 4 or less	67.6	22.2	68.2	71.4	62.7
	100.0%	100.0%	100.0%	100.0%	100.0%

$X^2 = 14.55$ Significance = .0022

TABLE 40

Liability Self-Insurance Index

		Industry Group			
	Manufac-turing	Transportation/Utilities	Wholesale/Retail Trade	Others	All Companies
Scores over 4	47.3%	77.8%	45.5%	50.0%	51.4%
Scores of 4 or less	52.7	22.2	54.5	50.0	48.6
	100.0%	100.0%	100.0%	100.0%	100.0%

$X^2 = 5.86$ Significance = .1194

---

[3] It is possible for scores to cluster about the median, with more than one subject scoring exactly on the breakpoint. Where all possible scores are integer number and such clustering occurs, the true median will be some integer plus a fraction. For example, the median for the property index is 4.18. No company may score exactly 4.18; therefore 4 is used as the breakpoint. In this case, 40% of the firms scored 4, making a division of approximately 50% both above and below the median impossible.

In order to assess the significance of the 32.4% under "Manufacturing," for example, the reader then, should compare it with the 37.3% in the "All Companies" column rather than with 50%.

Multiple Linear Regression Analysis

If all of the size and industry descriptors can be shown to be individually related to the self-insurance indexes, it should be possible to learn more about the characteristics of self-insuring firms.

A statistical technique commonly used to describe the effect of a group of variables on another variable is called multiple linear regression. Applied to this case, the aim is to determine the collective impact of our categories of size and industry classification on the self-insurance index. The self-insurance index will be treated as the dependent variable, and industry classification, annual revenue, total assets and number of employees, among other variables, will be treated as independent variables.

Brief mention should be made of the procedure used for including industry classification in this analysis. All of the other variables used in these multiple regression analyses are classed as "interval." For example, the value used for a firm's annual revenue, total assets or number of employees theoretically could lie anywhere on a positive number scale. But in the case of industry classification, a firm is in one class and only one class. That is, it is either a utility or it is not a utility. There is no range of values possible. To consider the effect of industry classification on the self-insurance index, we constructed three "dummy" variables. These variables were assigned the following values:

	Yes	No
Manufacturing (MANUFAC)	1	0
Transportation/Utility (TRANS)	1	0
Wholesale/Retail Trade (TRADE)	1	0

It can be seen that a firm will have a value of "1" for only one of these variables and "0" for both of the others if it is in one of these three groups. Otherwise it will have a "0" for all three variables.

One of the questions that might be asked is, "If we have specific information regarding a firm's size, does this information tell us anything about that firm's propensity to self-insure?" The process of choosing the independent variables to be related to the dependent variable is often called "specification." One specification has the overall self-insurance index (SIINDEX 1) as the dependent variable and industry classification, revenue (SALES), assets (ASSETS), and number of employees (NOFEMP) as the independent variables. The correlation matrix (Table 41) indicates that the overall index has the highest correlation with the size measures of revenues, assets and number of employees. The correlation between the index and a firm's position in the manufacturing group or the wholesale/retail trade group is sufficiently weak that these variables can be expected to be of little use in the regression equation. Note that while the correlation between trade and the index is actually negative, it is so close to zero that we cannot assume either a negative or a positive correlation.

TABLE 41

Correlations[4] among Revenue, Assets, Number of Employees, Industry Classification and the Overall Self-Insurance Index

	SIINDEX1	TRADE	TRANS	MANUFAC	NOFEMP	ASSETS	SALES
SALES	.26	–.11	.04	–.13	.89	.53	1.0
ASSETS	.23	–.16	.12	–.19	.41	1.0	.53
NOFEMP	.29	–.09	–.04	.18	1.0	.41	.89
MANUFAC	.07	–.45	–.43	1.0	.18	–.19	.13
TRANS	.14	–.17	1.0	–.43	–.04	.12	.04
TRADE	–.02	1.0	–.17	–.45	–.09	–.16	–.11
SIINDEX1	1.0	–.02	.14	.07	.29	.23	.26

The regression equation which results from this specification suggests the following. Knowing either a firm's revenue or its total assets tells as much about its propensity to self-insure as knowing both. A firm's revenue and its number of employees are so strongly correlated that only one of these variables may be used in the equation—one will do as well as the other. If we know that a firm is a transportation or utility company, we can expect it to be somewhat more likely to self-insure than if it is in some other business. We gain little from knowing a firm's industry classification if it is not in the transportation and utility category. Knowing all this information, we could expect to be able to predict a firm's exact score on the self-insurance index 13% of the time, on the average.

By experimenting with various other specifications (combinations of independent variables), including net income and profitability in addition to the ones already mentioned, we attempted to improve our ability to describe the interrelationships between those data which measure a firm's size, and other attributes, and its relative involvement in self-insurance. Our success waxed and waned with various specifications.

---

[4] A correlation is a measure of the tendency of pairs of values, for example x and y, to move together. A perfect positive relationship (a coefficient of +1.0) indicates that if x increases by one unit, the corresponding y value also increases by one unit. A perfect negative correlation (−1.0) says a one-unit increase in x results in a one-unit decrease in the corresponding y value. Less than perfect correlations can range anywhere between +1.0 and −1.0 with a correlation coefficient of 0.0 indicating values do not move together at all. The correlation matrix is simply a table showing the correlations between every possible pairing of the variables used in multiple regression.

If our object were, in fact, to find a single mathematical equation that could be used to estimate a firm's self-insurance score from knowledge of its industry group, its size, and its profitability, we would have to admit failure. On the other hand, if our intent were to examine these interrelationships and measure their strength and significance statistically, we were successful. In the process we discovered that self-insuring firms are diverse and our ability to categorize them is not improved by considering all of the classification data together using multiple regression techniques.

Our inability to devise a single tool for describing self-insurers does not detract from the knowledge gained from applying less complex statistical tests to the relationships between the self-insurance indexes and the measures of size, and so on, taken singly. In this regard we have shown that relative involvement in every area of self-insurance except workers' compensation has a significant relationship to a firm's size. (The workers' compensation exception is not unexpected because all respondents are large enough to have a sufficient number of employees to make self-insurance of this risk feasible.) It also is clear that firms in the transportation/utility group are likely to get more heavily into self-insurance than are those in other industries.

How Relative Levels of Involvement Relate to Other Items of Interest

We also were interested in the subject of how relative levels of involvement in self-insurance relate to other items of interest previously discussed in other chapters in different contexts.

For heavier self-insurers, as shown by the overall index, specific self-insurance decisions are made more often by insurance managers than for firms with a lesser involvement in self-insurance. This finding was not surprising given that the level of self-insurance involvement is related to size and that larger firms are more likely to have an insurance manager. It also appears to be true that regardless of the firm's size, if decisions involving choices between self-insurance and other risk management techniques are assigned to a risk management professional, the decision is more likely to favor heavy involvement in self-insurance than if such decisions are vested in another person.

Firms with heavier self-insured risks are much more likely to be influenced by the availability of qualified personnel to administer the self-insurance program. It also appears from the information collected that if heavily self-insured firms had additional qualified personnel, they would self-insure even more.

We found nonavailability of commercial insurance to be related to the score on the self-insurance index. This relationship probably emerges because of the greater likelihood of transportation and utility firms finding commercial insurance to be unavailable on jet airliners and nuclear power plants.

With regard to both property and liability risks, heavy self-insurers are much more likely to increase their self-insurance in the next five years than are those who are not already heavily involved.

To close this chapter, we present a profile of selected firms—according to their scores on the overall self-insurance index. Many of the relationships we have discussed will be readily apparent in this tabular presentation on pages 72 and 73.

Overall Self-Insurance Index — Top, Middle and Bottom Scorers

Case No.[1]	Industry Classification	Overall S-I Index (Maximum Possible—56)	Size Category[2]			Score in Other S-I Indexes		
			Revenue	Assets	Employees	Property (Maximum Possible—20)	Liability (Maximum Possible—16)	Workers' Compensation & Employee Benefits (Maximum Possible—20)
The Top 10								
168	Utility	39	1	1	1	13	9	17
167	Utility	38	1	1	2	10	12	16
59	Manufacturing	35	1	1	2	20	4	11
183	Retail	35	3	4	2	20	12	3
186	Utility	33	3	2	5	13	12	8
116	Manufacturing	31	2	2	3	16	0	15
13	Manufacturing	30	1	1	1	5	9	16
159	Manufacturing	30	1	1	1	17	9	4
63	Mining	29	2	2	3	13	8	8
191	Utility	29	5	4	5	11	9	9
The Middle 10, plus ties								
21	Finance	15	2	1	3	4	3	8
83	Manufacturing	15	3	4	4	4	3	8
149	Service	15	5	5	4	4	3	8
189	Manufacturing	15	3	3	2	8	4	3
193	Service	15	6	6	6	4	8	3
4	Service	14	4	6	6	4	3	7
5	Service	14	3	3	3	4	6	4
73	Manufacturing	14	5	5	5	4	1	9
92	Utility	14	1	1	2	8	3	3
103	Manufacturing	14	3	4	3	0	12	2
181	Manufacturing	14	3	4	3	4	4	6

Overall Self-Insurance Index — Top, Middle and Bottom Scorers

Case No.[1]	Industry Classification	Overall S-I Index (Maximum Possible—56)	Size Category[2]			Score in Other S-I Indexes		
			Revenue	Assets	Employees	Property (Maximum Possible—20)	Liability (Maximum Possible—16)	Workers' Compensation & Employee Benefits (Maximum Possible—20)
The Bottom 10, plus ties								
17	Utility	4	2	2	4	0	3	1
51	Manufacturing	4	1	1	1	0	0	4
66	Retail	4	5	5	4	3	0	1
69	Manufacturing	4	5	6	5	3	1	0
81	Service	4	4	4	4	4	0	0
112	Service	4	4	4	4	4	0	0
71	Manufacturing	3	5	5	5	0	0	3
93	Finance	3	6	1	4	2	1	0
130	Manufacturing	2	5	5	5	1	0	1
195	Manufacturing	2	6	6	6	1	1	0
115	Real Estate	1	5	5	6	0	1	0

(1) Case numbers were assigned in the order in which completed questionnaires were received.

(2) Size categories are scaled from 1 for largest to 6 for smallest.

Chapter 7

Summary and Recommendations

A majority of large American business firms self-insure a significant portion of the risks they face in the conduct of their operations. Of the 198 firms that completed and returned the questionnaire utilized in this study, 142 firms (over 70%) are using one or more of the four self-insurance techniques identified in the introduction to the questionnaire. Some of the firms are heavily involved in self-insurance, while others are into self-insuring only one type of risk such as health care or workers' compensation.

The larger the firm, the larger the involvement in self-insurance for property and liability risks. Self-insuring workers' compensation, health insurance and other employee benefit risks, however, is not concentrated in the largest companies but appears to be rather uniformly practiced by companies of various sizes. A logical conclusion appears to emerge— companies interested in experimenting with self-insurance may want to try it first in workers' compensation or health care. Usually it is feasible to segment the employee population by state, division, plant, or otherwise in order to initially self-insure only a portion of the total risk.

Many insurance brokers and agents have, in recent years, become ready, willing and able to assist their clients in setting up self-insurance programs. This phenomenon is probably a response to the sage advice, "If you can't beat them, join them." Regardless of the motivation, brokers and agents are definitely in the business of assisting their clients with self-insurance techniques as a part of their overall risk management programs. Business managers should not hesitate to discuss the self-insurance possibility with their brokers, agents, or other insurance professionals.

Managers who are considering the self-insurance possibility should keep in mind that they also can take a gradual approach with respect to the *degree* of risk taking. They could start by raising the deductibles on some or all of their commercial policies and then, over a period of years—depending on their experience—move into formal self-insurance programs and possibly captive insurance companies. Only occasionally will a company assume 100% of a significant risk. It can, and probably should, arrange for a commercial insurance company to assume the risk beyond the amount the company can realistically handle purchasing a "stop loss" or "excess coverage" policy.

Appendix A

Previous Studies

There have been several other studies on various aspects of self-insurance. We have reviewed five of them and have summarized their findings in this appendix.

Year Published	Researcher	Sponsor	Self-Insurance Emphasis
1964	Goshay	The S.S. Heubner Foundation for Insurance Education	Extent of self-insurance; accounting and funding; evaluation of costs and savings
1973	*Fortune* Market Research	Time, Inc.	Incidence and extent of self-insurance
1975	Unknown	*TIME* Magazine	Incidence and extent of self-insurance; use of outside consultants
1976	Hogue and Olson	Sentry Insurance Group	Risk identification and analysis; self-insurance decision; funding
1978	Goshay	Financial Accounting Standards Board	Impact on self-insurance decision of rule prohibiting contingency accounting accruals

The 1964 Goshay and the 1976 Hogue and Olson works are more extensive than others. They contain valuable textual material, whereas the other publications essentially are limited to compilations of survey findings. In the following paragraphs we shall summarize those findings of the earlier studies that are pertinent to the self-insurance decision.

Goshay, 1964

Robert Goshay's study of self-insurance, conducted while pursuing his doctorate at the University of Pennsylvania, remains the most significant treatise of the subject. The survey portion of his study was directed to the 150 members of the American Society of Insurance Management (now the Risk and Insurance Management Society, Inc.) who had indicated in an earlier mailing to all 1,100 ASIM member companies that they were utilizing self-insurance. Responses from 100 of the 150 self-insurers form the bases for the empirical portion of his study.

Highlights of Goshay's findings—referenced by his table numbers—are as follows:

6-3 Manufacturers were much less likely to retain the liability risk than were mining and construction; transportation, communication and public utilities; or wholesalers and retailers.

Industry classification appeared to have little bearing on the decision to retain fire risks and workers' compensation risks.

6-4 Large companies (over $749 million in assets) were much more likely to self-insure fire risk than small companies (under $50 million in assets). Medium-sized companies tend to be grouped with large companies.

Large companies also were much more likely to self-insure liability risk than small companies or medium-sized companies.

Size appeared to be of no consequence in the self-insurance decision on workers' compensation risks.

6-5 Exactly one-half of self-insured risks were backed up by "reserves," most of which were only "bookkeeping reserves."

Less than 10% of self-insured risks had funds set aside from which to pay losses.

6-6 Of those companies who maintained any type of self-insurance reserve, fewer than 10% based the size of the reserve on premiums they otherwise would have paid.

Most reserve additions were determined by judgment estimates based on previous years' losses.

7-1 Only one-half of the respondents made any attempt to keep track of the expenses incident to their self-insurance programs.

7-2 Fewer than one-half of the respondents computed how much they were saving by self-insuring.

8-1 Almost two-thirds of the companies self-insuring fire risks operated in 20 or more separate locations.

8-2 There was little discernable relationship between the size of deductibles in fire insurance policies and the size of the company, as measured by the dollar amount of assets exposed to fire loss.

More than half of the deductibles were in the $10,000-$20,000 range. (Those under $10,000 were not tabulated.)

8-3 Of the firms self-insuring liability risks, three-fourths had total assets of $125 million or more. (Twenty years ago, remember, that was a much larger sum than it is now.)

Goshay summarized some of his findings as follows:

a) **Financial Capacity** - Respondents kept well within their financial capacities in determining how much risk to retain.
b) **Exposure Distribution** - Respondents did not have the degree of loss stability which might be expected in self-insurers. Annual losses of the majority fluctuated more than 50% from the average of the previous three years.
c) **Catastrophe Protection** - All but about 15% of the risks retained by respondents were limited by catastrophe coverage. Only a few of the firms not purchasing catastrophe coverage had exposures which were suspect as to adequacy of mass, homogeneity and independence.

Fortune, 1973

Fortune directed its mail survey to chief executive officers of 500 of the nation's largest industrial corporations—250 from the "Top 500" and 250 from the "2nd 500." The 65% response rate was excellent.

The *Fortune* survey dealt mainly with the corporation's business with and knowledge of the insurance industry as exemplified by 25 large insurance companies and 11 large insurance brokers. Highlights of *Fortune's* findings relative to self-insurance are as follows:

- Approximately 75% of the largest industrial companies self-insured some part of their corporate risk.
- Said companies, on the average, self-insured approximately 10% of their risk (about 10% of the companies self-insured 25% or more of their risk).
- Approximately 52% of respondents expected to increase the portion of their risk handled by self-insurance.

TIME, 1975

A joint venture of *TIME* magazine and The Risk and Insurance Management Society, this survey was of the 1,786 RIMS members, up from 1,100 when Goshay circularized them 15 years earlier. After the usual follow-up mailings, *TIME* achieved a response rate of 50.9%, representing 909 completed questionnaires.

Highlights of the *TIME* study as regards self-insurance follow:

- In order to make property risk coverage more economical, about 45% of respondents had increased self-insurance in the preceding three years, and about 75% had increased the deductibles in their commercial policies.
- Percentages of companies' total insurable risk self-insured were as follows:

	None	1-24%	25-49%	50% and Over	(% of Respondents Answering)
Property	16	64	10	10	(69)
Liability	35	44	8	13	(64)
Employee benefits	46	21	4	29	(54)
All risks	16	52	16	16	(35)

- Of the companies using packaged services for self-insurance administration, the percentages using various resources were as follows:

	Carrier	Broker	Consultants and Independent Suppliers	Company Personnel	Other
Property	15	8	6	40	6
General liability	27	13	10	22	4
Owner liability	24	12	7	19	3
Workers' compensation	10	9	21	29	13
Employee benefits	29	14	21	26	7

(Percentages are not meaningful in themselves but are useful in assessing the relative usages of the various resources for self-insurance administration.)

- Thirty-nine companies (4.6%) had nine or more professional personnel in their risk/insurance department.

Hogue and Olson, 1976

This study was conducted by personal interviews of business executives responsible for risk and insurance matters. The sample was stratified so as to get adequate observations in each of five company sizes and each of six industrial classifications. Executives of 1,143 businesses were interviewed by Louis Harris and Associates, said businesses having been selected at random—subject to the stratification constraints—from a population of more than three million businesses in the data file of a nationally known reference service. Most of the companies included in the Hogue and Olson study were much smaller than those included in our study and the other studies previously discussed.

Highlights of the Hogue and Olson study, titled "Business Attitudes Toward Risk Management, Insurance and Related Social Issues," which relate directly to self-insurance follow.

- More than half of the businesses were involved in self-insurance, in the broad sense, in that they stated that they deliberately decided to absorb certain potential losses.
- More than 80% of the businesses did not have reserves for losses specifically earmarked. (Nondeductibility for tax purposes and nonaccruability for financial reporting purposes were not significant reasons for not having reserves.)
- Approximately 90% of the businesses not self-insuring thought that having insurance company services was more important than estimating savings from self-assumption.
- There was a tendency for business to "move away from self-insurance" in that a significantly larger percentage of companies raised the amount of insurance coverage than increased the size of the deductibles in such coverage.
- Four times as many large firms (sales over $25 million) as small firms were making greater use of self-insurance.
- The companies who were moving toward self-insurance were asked a "why" question similar to the thrust of some of the questions in our study. The reasons expressed by the Hogue and Olson companies were as shown by Table 42 on page 82, reproduced with their permission.

Goshay, 1978

This study was sponsored by the Financial Accounting Standards Board because of its concern about the possibility of its pronouncements having significant economic impacts in the business community, as distinguished from the intended accounting impacts.

Professor Goshay was retained to study the economic effects, if any, of FASB Statement No. 5, "Accounting for Contingencies," FASB, 1975—in particular whether the Statement had caused firms to make unsound risk and insurance management decisions.

Statement No. 5 ruled that, before a loss contingency may be recognized

TABLE 42

Reasons for Increasing Self-Insurance

	Major Reason	Minor Reason	Not A Reason At All	Total
Insurance companies excessively load the premium for expenses and profits	37.5%	18.1%	44.3%	99.9*%
Self-insurance forces your managers and employees to undertake more extensive loss prevention activities	34.9	17.8	47.2	99.9*
Self-insurance gives you better control over your cash flows	33.2	19.4	47.4	100.0
The insurance rate structure discriminates against your company as the underwriters are unwilling to adjust the rate to fit your particular situation	27.5	21.4	51.1	100.0
Coverage for all of your exposures is not available	13.6	14.1	72.3	100.0

*Error due to rounding

by a charge to income, both of the following conditions must be met:

1) It is probable that an asset *had* been impaired or a liability *had* been incurred at the data of the financial statements. (Emphasis added.)
2) The amount of loss can be reasonably estimated.

Because insurance reserves and related expense accruals have as their very nature cushioning for the financial statements against potential *future* adverse events, FASB Statement No. 5 clearly outlaws such reserves.

A natural concern developed as to whether the inability to spread expected self-insurance losses more or less evenly to income statements by periodic accruals would cause businesses to reduce their involvement with self-insurance and move toward carrying more commercial insurance, perhaps at increased cost. Dr. Goshay's study determined that such was not the case.

Goshay's respondents (approximately 160) indicated overwhelmingly that Statement No. 5 had little or no effect on anything they did outside the accounting function. On the strength of Goshay's study and finding, this accounting-related matter was relegated to a minor position in our study.

Appendix B

Case Study of Company New to Self-Insurance

Acme Corporation[1] is a manufacturer of hand tools such as wrenches, pliers, hammers and drills. It is headquartered in Harrisburg, Pa., where it has three plants. There are 12 other plants in 10 other cities plus a distribution center in Indianapolis, Ind. Steel is by far the major raw material of Acme, but it does operate one small wood mill.

Annual sales revenues of Acme are in the $200 million range and are divided almost equally between the "do-it-yourself" market and the industrial market. None of its plants employs more than 500 employees, most of which are unionized.

Insurance cost would not be considered a "big ticket" item for Acme. Until recently, Acme did not give major attention to its insurance cost, relying on the local office of a nationally known broker to handle practically all of its insurance matters. The president and financial vice-president exercised general surveillance over the broker's activities—to the degree required to satisfy themselves that Acme's risks were being insured adequately. The treasurer maintained liaison with the broker to the extent of informing the broker of new plants, new company cars, and the like. Beyond that, it was up to the broker to decide what to insure, how much to insure it for, and with whom to insure it.

Acme got into self-insurance more or less by accident, which probably is true of many companies. In Acme's case, it all began with ERISA (Employees Retirement Income Security Act). When Acme's lawyers and CPA s met with its financial vice-president to go over the reporting and other requirements of ERISA and how much they were going to need to raise their fees to handle all the extra work, the financial vice-president opined, "It looks as if we had better develop an in-house expert." (Acme actually had more retirement plans than it had plants.) Finding no one at the home office to assign, Acme's management decided to bring one of its experienced plant

---

[1] Names, places, products, and other facts have been changed at the request of the subject company.

managers, John Milburn, in from the field. Prior to joining Acme, Milburn had been assistant general manager of a large operation of another company where his responsibilities included personnel matters. In the process of wading through all the ERISA reporting requirements, Milburn undertook the task of consolidating or conforming various retirement plans, where possible, in order to make their administration more manageable. He gradually got involved in related "people costs" such as life insurance, health and accident insurance and workers' compensation insurance.

With the backing of Acme's top management, Milburn arranged the self-insuring of the workers' compensation risk in three of the nine states in which it operates. Acme consulted with a leading risk management consulting firm and several companies experienced in self-insurance before going into the program. They now have contracted with a leading self-insurance service firm to administer the processing of claims. Financial results to date, partially projected estimates, are as shown in Schedule 1. Approximately one-half of Acme's production workers are included in the self-insurance program. There are certain complications involved in the other six states, but plans are under way to self-insure the workers' compensation risk in three additional states where there are enough employees to make it feasible.

SCHEDULE 1

Self-Insured Workers' Compensation Program

	7/1/78-6/30/79	7/1/79-6/30/80
Quoted Cost of Commercial Insurance	$525,000	$852,000
	(One state)	(Three states)
Cost of Self-Insurance:		
Corporate Administration	25,000	40,000
Excess Insurance (incl. Aircraft)	113,000	140,000
Specific: $2 million Limits		
Aggregate: $1 million Limits		
Claims Administration	25,000	52,000
Loss Prevention Service	11,000	24,000
Total Fixed Cost	$174,000	$256,000
Estimated Total Losses	115,000	193,000
Estimated State Taxes	9,000	18,000
Total Cost*	$298,000	$467,000
Projected Savings	$227,000	$385,000

*Note: No allowance has been made for the value of increased cash flows or the detriment of postponed income tax deductions, which would tend to be offsetting.

After getting into self-insurance for workers' compensation, Milburn turned his attention to the health care risks Acme had contractually or otherwise become liable for. To date, approximately 25% of the health care exposure has been self-insured. Specifically, there is no commercial basic or major medical coverage for any of the 600 salaried employees or for 240 hourly employees in four plants. The experience to date is not conclusive because of such a short history, but it is sufficiently encouraging (Schedule 2) that approximately 700 hourly employees at other plants have been added since October 1, 1979. Catastrophe coverage is provided through an individual and aggregate stop-loss policy.

SCHEDULE 2

Self-Insured Health Care Program
Progress Report

Nine Months ended October 1, 1979

PARTICIPANTS

Salaried		600
Hourly:		
Plant A	40	
Plant B	20	
Plant C	150	
Plant D	30	240
Total		840
PRO-FORMA PREMIUMS*	$390,000	
CLAIMS	$278,600	
Experience (Claims to Premiums)		71.4%
ADMINISTRATIVE FEES	$ 31,400	
Experience (Claims and Fees to Premiums)		79.5%

*Note: Pro forma premiums amount is stated conservatively because it does not reflect increased benefit level or rate increase during plan year.

Acme also self-insures collision and comprehensive risks on all its trucks, vans and automobiles and is in the final stages of a feasibility study which, Milburn believes, will lead to formation of an offshore captive to handle most liability and property risks.

It would be very interesting to learn whether Acme is as enthusiastic about self-insurance five years into the program as it is now after about one year.

Appendix C

Topical Bibliography

I. Feasibility

Brockmeier, Warren G., "What to look for in captive company and self-insurance feasibility studies," Reprinted from *Risk Management* in *Self-Insurance, a Compendium of Articles.*

———————————, "Self-insurance vs. insurance for larger cities," *Municipal Finance,* (August 1971), pp. 14-21.

Brown, Bernard M., "Malpractice risk financing: the options," *Risk Management,* (July 1977), p. 24, ff.

Carnescchi, Ralph, "Is self-insurance answer to rising costs?", Reprinted from *Health Care Week.*

Daenzer, Bernard J., "Critical considerations in self-insurance programs," *Best's Review,* (Property/casualty edition, May 1977), p. 28, ff.

Daly, Walter M., "Some comments on self-insurance," *Arthur Young Journal,* (January 1963), pp. 11-18.

Fannin, Rebecca A., "Brokers continue to expand their services," *Business Insurance,* (May 29, 1978), pp. 17-18.

Geisel, Jerry, "Insurers fight tax breaks for self-insured reserves," *Business Insurance,* (May 29, 1978), p. 1, ff.

———————————, "Second bill proposes tax breaks for self-insurers," *Business Insurance,* (June 27, 1977), p. 6.

Gentry, Ralph E., "Assessing a company's ability to self-assume risk," Reprinted from *Risk Management* in *Self-Insurance, a Compendium of Articles.*

Goshay, Robert C., *Corporate Self Insurance and Risk Retention Plans,* (Richard D. Irwin, Inc., 1964).

Greene, Mark R., "Quantitative methods: a primer for risk managers," *Risk Management,* (July 1976), pp. 62-64.

———————————, *Risk and Insurance,* 4th edition, (Southwestern Publishing Company, 1977).

Hoare, W. A. D., "Self-funding insurance programs: are they practical?", *Credit and Financial Management,* (October 1969), p. 16, ff.

Kirchner, Merian, "These doctors have self-insured for five years now," *Medical Economics,* (November 1, 1976), p. 113, ff.

Kloman, H. Felix, "Risk financing in a chaotic market," Reprinted from *Risk Management* in *Self-Insurance, a Compendium of Articles.*

Krakowiecke, Marie, "Self-insurance? Choice of experts is largest ever," *Business Insurance,* (May 30, 1977), pp. 17-18.

_____, "Self-insuring? Excess markets may be crucial," *Business Insurance,* (February 7, 1977), pp. 8-9.

Lenz, Matthew Jr., *Risk Management Manual,* (The Merritt Company, Santa Monica, Calif., 1976).

"Little tax impact seen for self-insurance plan," *Business Insurance,* (June 12, 1978), p. 12.

"Lloyd's specialist wants oil industry to ease its self-insurance practices," *Business Insurance,* (October 4, 1976), p. 19.

Moore, Richard O., "The pros and cons of self-insurance." *Administrative Management,* (June 1978), pp. 34-35.

"Municipal liability in California: how it stands," *Risk Management,* (September 1976), pp. 46-50.

"New trends in underwriting reinsurance and risk management indicate that the market will never be the same again," *Insurance Marketing,* (May 1978), pp. 12-13.

"Optimistic excess view challenged," *Business Insurance,* (May 30, 1977), p. 75.

Ralston, August, "FASB Standard No. 5: a step backward?", *Risk Management,* (November 1975), pp. 42-44.

"Risk Retention," *Practical Risk Management,* (WMGH Corporation, 1975), No. A-12, pp. 1-7.

Roos, Nester R., "Self-insurance and other alternatives for financing risk," *Governmental Finance,* (May 1977), pp. 13-17.

Roubinek, Gary W., "New standards for self-insured businesses," *Credit and Financial Management,* (October 1975), pp. 28-29.

"Self-insurance considerations," *Accountant,* (November 17, 1977), pp. 628-630.

Staubus, George J., "Nonaccounting for noninsurance," *Accounting Review,* (January 1961), pp. 406-408.

Tagman, Charles T. Jr., "Self-insurance: a financial approach," *Management Review,* (April 1978), pp. 33-34.

"To cut high premium costs, more firms and institutions are insuring themselves," *Wall Street Journal,* (April 14, 1978).

Treischmann, James S. and E. J. Leverett, Jr., "Self-insurance: who should use it?", *Business Horizons,* (October 1975), pp. 45-53.

II. Planning and Implementation

Brink, Stephen D., "Actuaries are crucial in self-funded health plans," *Business Insurance,* (June 13, 1977), pp. 29-30.

Crisafulli, Nino D., "Are you self-insured? Consider obligations to excess insurer." *Business Insurance,* (October 29, 1978), pp. 61-62.

Greene, Mark R., "Insurance and risk management in the electronic era," *Journal of Insurance,* (November/December 1977), pp. 22-26.

Jenkins, Robert L., "Third-party administrators can be rated," *Business Insurance,* (June 12, 1978), pp. 29-32.

"Self-insurance—a big opportunity," *National Underwriter,* (Property edition, May 26, 1978), pp. 57-65.

Simon, Ellis, "Risks from soup to nuts; grocer's stock in trade," *Business Insurance,* (May 29, 1978), pp. 83-84.

"Underwriters Salvage extends its services to self-insuring firms," *National Underwriter,* (Property edition, March 18, 1977), p. 18.

III. Captive Insurance Companies

"Captive insurance companies," *Practical Risk Management,* (WMGH Corporation, 1976), No. A-16, pp. 1-16.

Captive Insurance Company Reports, (Risk Planning Group, Inc., Darien, Conn.)

"Ford and the IRS are still in court over Bermuda captive transactions," *Business Insurance,* (May 29, 1978), p. 2.

Insurance Decisions: Captive Insurance Companies, (Insurance Company of North America.)

"Insure yourself?", *Forbes,* (September 15, 1976), p. 62.

McIntyre, Kathryn J., "Captive managing: basking in boom," *Business Insurance,* (September 4, 1978), p. 11, ff.

"Tennessee clarifies captive law," *Business Insurance,* (May 29, 1978), p. 2.

IV. Employee Benefits

Clarke, Warner B., "Can self-insurance save you dollars?", *Pension World,* (December 1978), pp. 56-60.

Greg, David, "Court case could set self-funded trust rules," *Business Insurance,* (April 18, 1977), p. 1, ff.

_____, "Congressional report backs state trust regulation," *Business Insurance,* (May 2, 1977), p. 14.

"Florida firms self-fund comp," *Business Insurance,* (May 29, 1978), p. 78.

Geisel, Jerry, "Florida firms pool and not a claim since April," *Business Insurance,* (June 12, 1978), p. 21.

Harber, Carlton, "Self-insurance: an employer's option." *Personnel Journal,* (May 1977), pp. 251-252.

Kelley, Robert E., "Self-funding a company's health benefit plans," *Pension World,* (March 1977), pp. 26-29.

Konigsberg, David, "Self-insured benefits spur ASO growth," *Business Insurance,* (May 30, 1977), pp. 11-12.

Meyer, Mitchell, "Cutting costs through self-insurance," *Conference Board Record,* (September 1976), pp. 36-38.

Moskal, B. S., "Health care savings via self-insurance," *Industry Week,* (June 12, 1978), p. 114, ff.

"Self-insurance is no insurance," *National Underwriter,* (June 24, 1978), p. 114.

Simon, Ellis, "Asher's benefit self-insurance plan means major impact on bottom line," *Business Insurance,* (May 29, 1978), pp. 87-88.

Sinclair-Whitely, Brian, "Cash flow funding and risk sharing of employee benefit programs," *Risk Management,* (July 1976), p. 20, ff.

Walter, D. H., "Tax changes effected by the Black Lung Benefits Act of 1977," *Taxes,* (May 1977), pp. 251-254.

"Workers' compensation self-insurance," *Practical Risk Management,* (WMGH Corporation, 1978), No. A-14, pp. 1-9.

V. Product Liability

Goshay, Robert C., "Economic impact of self-insurance reserve trusteed funds: product and general liability exposures," *Journal of Risk and Insurance,* (September 1977), pp. 521-526.

_____, "An overview of the products liability crisis," *Best's Review,* (Property/casualty edition, January 1978), p. 17, ff.

Scheibla, Shirley, "IRS to the rescue? Deductible insurance might cope with product liability," *Barron's,* (February 6, 1978), p. 11, ff.

"Tax breaks for reserves can only help," *Business Insurance,* (May 29, 1978), p. 8.

"The Devil's in the product liability laws," *Business Week,* (February 12, 1979), pp. 72-78.

VI. General

Goshay, Robert C., *Corporate Self-Insurance and Risk Retention Plans,* (Richard D. Irwin, Inc., Homewood, Ill., 1964).

Greene, Mark R., *Risk and Insurance,* (South-Western, 1977).

Risk Management Manual, (Merritt Company, Santa Monica, Calif.), (A loose-leaf service).

Business Insurance, (Crain Communication, Inc., Chicago, Ill.), (A newsweekly).

Risk Management, (Risk and Insurance Management Society, Inc.), (A monthly journal).

Best's Review— Property/Casualty Insurance Edition, (A.M. Best Co., Inc., Oldwick, N.J.), (A monthly journal).

(In addition to articles, the three periodicals at the end of the above list contain numerous advertisements of firms active in self-insurance consultation or assistance.)

Appendix D

Exposure Inventory

This appendix has been included in order to provide a more complete description of the procedures a firm may need to follow in order to fully identify the risks it faces.

The appendix comprises selected portions of the Exposure Inventory included in Merritt's[1] *Risk Management Manual* and is reproduced with their permission.

As shown on the following outline, five sections have been reproduced. Sections not reproduced are similar in format but different, of course, in content.

---

[1] Merritt Company, P.O. Box 955, Santa Monica, Calif. 90406.

ASSET — EXPOSURE ANALYSIS

LIST I — ASSETS

A. **PHYSICAL ASSETS OWNED OR FOR WHICH RESPONSIBLE**

1. **Real Property**

    a. Physical Structures (complete or under construction)
        - (1) Under Construction
        - (2) Manufacturing
        - (3) Offices
        - (4) Warehouses
        - (5) Garages and Hangars
        - (6) Dwellings and Farms
        - (7) Tanks, Towers and Stacks
        - (8) Wharfs and Docks
        - (9) Pipes and Wires (above ground)
        - (10) Bridges

    b. Underground Property
        - (1) Cables and Wires
        - (2) Tanks
        - (3) Shelters, Caves and Tunnels
        - (4) Mines and Shafts
        - (5) Wells, Ground Water
        - (6) Piping and Pipelines
        - (7) Mineral Deposits (solid, liquid, gas)

    c. Land
        - (1) Unimproved
        - (2) Quarries
        - (3) Bodies of Waste
        - (4) Dumps

2. **Personal Property (on and off premises and in transit)**

    a. Aircraft
        - (1) Fixed Wing — jet, piston, glider
        - (2) Rotary Wing
        - (3) Missiles and Satellites
        - (4) Lighter than Air

    b. Animals: Farm, Domestic (pets), Stock, Laboratory, Security

    c. Antennae, including Towers

    d. Crops, Gardens, Lawns, Shrubbery, Standing Timber

    e. Electronic Data Processing Equipment and Uninscribed Information Holding Devices

ASSET — EXPOSURE ANALYSIS

ASSETS

f. Equipment and Machinery

    (1) Machines and Tools
    (2) Dies, Jigs, Molds, Castings, Patterns and Plates
    (3) Boilers and Pressure Vessels

        (a) Fired Vessels — Steam and Hot Water Boilers
        (b) Unfired Vessels

    (4) Mechanical Electrical Equipment (transformers, generators, motors, fans, pumps, compressors)
    (5) Engines — diesel, gasoline, steam, electric
    (6) Meters and Gauges
    (7) Turbines — steam, gas, water
    (8) Conveyors and Lifts, Trams, Elevators, Escalators, Overhead Cranes
    (9) Furnaces, Ovens, Kilns

g. Fences

h. Fine Arts — antiques, paintings, jewelry, libraries

i. Furniture and Fixtures

j. Improvements and Betterments

k. Nuclear and Radioactive Materials — isotopes, tracers, reactors, cyclotrons, accelerators, bevatrons, by-product material

l. Precious Metals

m. Promotional Displays — signs, models, plates, handbills, exhibits, films

n. Recreational Facilities — parks, gyms, lakes, cafeterias, other

o. Security Protection and Detection Devices

p. Stock — supplies, raw materials, goods in process, finished goods

q. Valuable Records (include value of blank records, cost of having data inscribed and functional availability of data)

    (1) Blueprints
    (2) Formulae
    (3) Accounts Receivable
    (4) Patents and Copyrights
    (5) Titles and Deeds
    (6) Tapes, Cards, Discs, Programs
    (7) Own Securities — negotiable and non-negotiable
    (8) Other Securities — in own custody or in custody of others
    (9) Cash (including bank deposits)
    (10) Plates
    (11) Mortgages, Bond Indentures, Leases
    (12) Insurance Policies

r. Vehicles (including contents)

    (1) Commercial
    (2) Private Passenger
    (3) Contractors' Equipment (licensed)
    (4) Warehouse Equipment

s. Watercraft (including contents) — boats, yachts, barges, ships, submersibles, buoys, drilling rigs

B. **INTANGIBLE ASSETS** (assets not necessarily shown on Balance Sheet or Earnings Statement)

1. External Assets

    a. Markets

    b. Resource Availability

        (1) Finance — credit, currency convertibility
        (2) Suppliers
        (3) Transportation
        (4) Employees (full-time and temporary)
        (5) Public Utilities
        (6) Public Protection

    c. Communications — telephone, teletype, television, radio, newspaper, postal service

    d. Natural Environment — climate, geography, geology

    e. Physical Environment — neighbors, community access

    f. Economic Environment and Stability

    g. Social and Political Environment

    h. Availability of Counsel and Specialists — legal, architectural, accounting, insurance, real estate, general management, marketing, advertising, banking, public relations, engineering

2. Internal Assets

    a. Research and Development

    b. Goodwill and Reputation

    c. Financial

        (1) Credit with Suppliers
        (2) Credit Lines (received)
        (3) Insurance
        (4) Royalties and Rents
        (5) Leasehold Interest
        (6) Company Foundations (nonprofit)
        (7) Tax Loss Carry-Forward
        (8) Trusts [e.g. 501(c)(9)]

    d. Personnel (employees and executives)

        (1) Education and Training
        (2) Experience
        (3) "Key" Employees

    e. Rights

        (1) Mineral and Oil Rights, (above, underground and offshore)
        (2) Air Rights
        (3) Patents and Copyrights
        (4) Royalty Agreements

          (5)   Distribution Agreements
          (6)   Manufacturing Rights

   f.   Employee Benefit Plans

          (1)   Death Benefits
          (2)   Disability Income (Short-Term and Long-Term)
          (3)   Medical Plan: Health Maintenance Organizations
          (4)   Pensions
          (5)   Income Plans: Profit Sharing, Stock Purchase, Thrift
          (6)   Time Off with Pay: Holidays, Vacations, Sabbaticals
          (7)   Payroll Deduction Insurance: Life/Accident, Property/Casualty
          (8)   Special Facilities: Dining, Expenses, Company Cars, Credit

ASSET — EXPOSURE ANALYSIS

LIST II — EXPOSURES TO LOSS

A. DIRECT EXPOSURES

1. Breakage of Glass — other fragile items
2. Breakdown — malfunction of part, lubricant, etc.
3. Collision — on and off premises, watercraft, aircraft, vehicle
4. Contamination — liquid, solid, gaseous, radioactive, pollution
5. Corrosion — wear, tear, abuse, poor maintenance
6. Electrical Disturbance — lightning, burnout, sun spots, power surge, demagnetization of magnetic recording devices
7. Employee Dishonesty — forgery, embezzlement, larceny, theft
8. Employee Negligence
9. Explosion and Implosion
10. Failure of Environmental Control — temperature, humidity, pressure
11. Falling Objects — aircraft, meteors, missiles, trees
12. Fauna — animals, rodents, insects, pests
13. Fire
14. Fraud, Forgery, Theft, Burglary, Robbery
15. Installation and Construction Hazards — dropping
16. Intentional Destruction — jettison, backfiring, etc.
17. Invalidity of Deed, Title, Patent, Copyright
18. Inventory Shortage — mysterious disappearance, lost or mislaid property
19. Land Movement — earthquake, volcano, landslide, avalanche
20. Obsolescence
21. Order of Civil Authority — expropriation, demolition, nationalization, seizure, exercise of eminent domain, confiscation, escheat laws, garnishment of payroll
22. Perils of Sea — pirates, rovers, barratry, etc.
23. Physical Change — shrinkage, evaporation, color, mildew, rot, expansion, contraction, deterioration
24. Riots, Civil Disorders, Strikes, Boycotts, Curfews
25. Rupture, Puncture of Tank, Vessel
26. Smoke Damage Smudge
27. Sound and Shock Waves — sonic boom, vibration, water hammer
28. Spillage, Leakage, Paint Spray
29. Structural Defects
30. Subsidence — collapse, settlement, erosion

31. Transportation – overturn, collision
32. Unintentional Error – employee, computer, counsel, etc.
33. Vandalism, Malicious Mischief, Defacing of Property
34. War, Insurrection, Rebellion, Armed Revolt, Sabotage
35. Water Damage – flood, rising waters, flash flood, mudslide, tidal wave (tsunami), geyser, ground water, sprinkler leakage, sewer back-up
36. Weight of Ice, Snow
37. Windstorm – typhoon, hurricane, cyclone, tornado, hailstorm, rain, dust, seiche, sandstorm

B. **INDIRECT OR CONSEQUENTIAL EXPOSURES**

1. All Direct Exposures as They Affect:
   a. Suppliers and Creditors
   b. Customers
   c. Utilities
   d. Transportation (personnel and property)
   e. Employees

2. Bankruptcy – employee, executive, supplier, customer, counselor

3. Change in Style, Taste, Desire

4. Concentration of Assets

5. Disruption of Educational System (racial, political, economic)

6. Economic Fluctuation – inflation, recession, depression

7. Epidemic, Disease, Plague, Quarantine

8. Extra Expense – rentals, communication, product, etc.

9. Increased Replacement Cost, Depreciation

10. Inter- and Intra-facility Dependency

11. Invasion of Copyright, Patent

12. Loss of Integral Part of Set, Pair, Group

13. Loss of Rights Resulting from Records Destruction

14. Managerial Error in:
    a. Pricing, Marketing
    b. Distribution
    c. Production
    d. Expansion
    e. Economic Predictions
    f. Political Predictions
    g. Investments
    h. Dividend Declaration
    i. Tax Filing

15. Recall of Product

16. Spoilage

Appendix
Supplement #26 – 5/76
(Supersedes Supplement #1)

C.   **THIRD PARTY LIABILITIES (compensatory and punitive damages)**

1.   Advertiser's and Publisher's Liability

   a.   As Agents
   b.   Libel, Slander, Defamation of Character
   c.   Media Used — radio, TV, newspaper, samples, exhibits

2.   Athletic — sponsorship of teams, recreational facilities, etc.

3.   Automobile Liability

   a.   Operation of Vehicles — owned and non-owned
   b.   Loading and Unloading
   c.   Dangerous Contents — flammables, explosives
   d.   Garagekeeper's Liability

4.   Aviation Liability

   a.   Owned and Leased Aircraft
   b.   Non-owned — officers and employees licensed
   c.   Grounding and Sistership Liability
   d.   Hangar Owner's Legal Liability

5.   Bailee Liability

6.   Care, Custody and Control of Property of Others

7.   Contractual Liability

   a.   Purchase Agreements
   b.   Sales Agreements
   c.   Lease Agreements — real or personal property
   d.   Performance or Service
   e.   Loans, Mortgages, Notes
   f.   Hold Harmless Clauses
   g.   Surety Agreements
   h.   Construction

8.   Director's and Officers Liability (stockholder derivative suits)

9.   Easements

   a.   In Gross
   b.   Appurtenant
   c.   Positive or Negative Under Common Law
   d.   Rights to Access to Light, Water, Drainage, Support

10.   Employer's Liability

   a.   Workers' Compensation or Similar Laws
   b.   Federal Employees Liability Act
   c.   Common Law
   d.   U.S. Longshoremen's and Harbor Worker's Act
   e.   Jones Act
   f.   Defense Bases Act
   g.   Outer Continental Shelf Act
   h.   Unemployment Compensation
   i.   Discrimination in Employment

      j.   Economic Opportunity Act
      k.   Voluntary Compensation Agreements
      l.   Equal Opportunity Act

11. Fringe Benefit Plans Liability

      a.   Pensions, Trusts, Profit Sharing Plans, Investments
      b.   Insured — life, accident, health, etc.
      c.   Credit Unions

12. Liquor Law or Dram Shop Act Liability

13. Malpractice Liability — Errors and Omissions

      a.   Medical — doctors, nurses, specialists
      b.   Legal and Tax
      c.   Engineering and Architectural
      d.   Trustees of Pension Plans
      e.   Patent Infringement
      f.   Data Processing
      g.   Accounting
      h.   Consulting
      i.   Travel and Insurance Agency

14. Non-Ownership Liability

      a.   Leased Real or Personal Property
      b.   Bailee's Liability
      c.   Employee's Use of Vehicle, Aircraft, Watercraft

15. Ordinary Negligence

      a.   Of Employees
      b.   Of Agents
      c.   Of Invited or Uninvited Guests
      d.   Of Contractor or Subcontractor
      e.   Failure to Provide Safety Equipment, Warnings, etc.
      f.   Inadequate Enforcement of Regulations
      g.   Improper Preparation of Food

16. Owner's Liability

      a.   Attractive Nuisance
      b.   Invited Guests
      c.   Trespassers (false arrest)
      d.   Rights of Others — riparian, mineral, light, air, view, lateral support, easements, part walls, licenses, drainage, eminent domain

17. Personal Injury

      a.   Libel
      b.   Slander
      c.   Defamation of Character
      d.   Piracy
      e.   False Arrest
      f.   Misuse of Legal Process

g.   Imprisonment
h.   Mental Anguish
i.   Shock
j.   Fright
k.   Detention
l.   Eviction
m.   Malicious Prosecution
n.   Invasion of Privacy
o.   Wrongful Entry
p.   Discrimination
q.   Humiliation
r.   Loss of Reputation

18. Product Liability (each product sold, distributed, made)

   a.   Implied Warranty
   b.   Express Warranty

       (1)   By Agents — sales, advertising or general
       (2)   By Employees
       (3)   Of Merchantability
       (4)   Of Suitability or Fitness for Use
       (5)   Of Title
       (6)   By Sample

19. Protective Liability

   a.   Industrial Contractors Hired
   b.   Construction or Demolition

20. Railroad Liability

   a.   Sidetrack Agreements
   b.   Right-of-Way
   c.   Grade Crossings
   d.   Federal Employer's Liability Act

21. Watercraft Liability

   a.   Ownership, Leased, Operation
   b.   Types — boats, yachts, ships, submersibles

Appendix
Supplement #26 — 5/76
(Supersedes Supplement #1)

PLANT MANAGEMENT

Company: _____ Date: _____

(NOTE: Complete a separate form for each plant location.)

1. Plant name and type: _____

   _____

2. Plant address: _____

   _____

3. Key personnel:

   A. Plant Manager _____

   B. Personnel Director _____

   C. Safety Director _____

   D. Cashier _____

   E. Purchasing Agent _____

   F. Other _____

4. Plant Manager's estimate of probable maximum loss:

   A. Loss of physical property

      (1) building _____

      (2) fixtures and equipment _____

      (3) stock and inventory _____

   B. Loss of earnings _____

   C. Third party liability _____

5. Adjacent exposures:

   A. North _____

   B. East _____

   C. South _____

   D. West _____

Any explosion hazard on adjacent properties? _____

_____

6. Operations:

	Number of Months	Number of Shifts	Days per Week	Days of No Operations
A.	_____	_____	_____	_____

B. Are operations seasonal? _____

C. Peak periods _____

D. Total plant employees _____

E. Turnover _____

F. Local unemployment rate _____

G. Is any special training necessary for employees? _____

H. If so, what is the average length of training time? _____

7. Description of operations:

A. Raw Materials

    Type _____

    Storage _____

    How received _____

B. Process

    Type _____

C. Products

    Type _____

    Storage _____

    How shipped _____

8. General administration:

   A. Care and housekeeping _____

   B. Maintenance _____

   C. Fencing _____

   D. Smoking and fire safety regulations _____

   E. Storage of flammable materials _____

   F. Use of radioactive or fissionable materials _____

9. Do you have any key employees (individually or as a group) whose death or total disablement would result in substantial financial loss?

Name	Potential Loss ($)

10. Plant protection:

    A. *Plant water system*

Size of Mains	Type of Grid	Supply	No. of Hydrants

    Is fire system connected to process water? _____

    _____

    B. *Fire Pumps*

Type	Size	Drive	Source of Supply

EXPOSURE INVENTORY

PLANT MANAGEMENT

C.   *Water reserves or tanks*

Type	Volume	Elevation
_____	_____	_____
_____	_____	_____
_____	_____	_____

D.   *Water tests*

Hyd. Loc.	Static PSI	GPM Flow	Residual PSI	Date of Test
_____	_____	_____	_____	_____
_____	_____	_____	_____	_____
_____	_____	_____	_____	_____

E.   *Auxiliary equipment*

Hose Houses	Amount of Hose
_____	_____
_____	_____
_____	_____

F.   *Sprinkler systems*

Type & Size of Valve	Area Covered	Type of System
_____	_____	_____
_____	_____	_____
_____	_____	_____

Is sprinkler system maintained by outside contractor? _____

Source of supply _____

Are all exposed areas protected from freezing? _____

G.   *Describe alarms and any supervisory service.* _____

_____

_____

Does central station service have key to premises? _____

H. *Standpipes*

                Location   **Size**

_____   _____

_____   _____

I. *Drain tests*

Valve Loc.	PSI Before Flow	PSI During Flow	PSI After Flow
_____	_____	_____	_____
_____	_____	_____	_____

J. *Fire extinguishers*

General Type	Distribution	Maintenance
_____	_____	_____
_____	_____	_____
_____	_____	_____

K. *Describe any other fixed protection.* _____

_____

_____

L. *Fire brigade*

Type Training	Amount	Number of Men
_____	_____	_____

M. *Watchman service*

Hours Covered	Period of Rounds	Watchclock	Number of Stations
_____	_____	_____	_____

Describe area or times not covered. _____

_____

_____

_____

11. Unusual exposures:

A. *Flood*

Relation of plant in distance and elevation to nearest rivers, streams or other bodies of water _____

_____

_____

_____

Previous experience of flood or water damage _____

_____

Have any precautions been provided by assured or others such as U. S. Corps of Engineers?

_____

_____

B. *Earthquake*

Earthquake zone rating _____

Previous history of earthquakes _____

_____

C. *Collapse*

Description of piers, wharfs or any abnormal structures _____

_____

_____

Is the plant or any building constructed on filled ground? _____

_____

When constructing buildings, are pilings used? _____

_____

Any past history of collapse? _____

D. *Other known perils*

_____

_____

BUILDING DATA

(Answer all questions separately for each building.)

Company: _____.   Date: _____

Location: _____

1. Construction:

   A.   Outside walls _____

   B.   Roof _____

   C.   Floors _____

2. Number of floors: _____

3. Floor area (get map of premises, if possible) _____

4. Frontage of building and lot _____

5. Name and address of mortgagee: _____

   _____

6. Amount and expiration of mortgage: _____.

7. Occupancy:

   A.   Portion occupied by insured _____

   B.   By others _____

8. If rented to others:

   A.   Is tenant liable for increase in fire rate on buildings? _____

   _____.

   B.   Is tenant required to carry

        Fire insurance in your favor? _____

        Liability insurance in your favor? _____

   C.   Obligations of tenant with regard to repairs and maintenance _____

   _____

EXPOSURE INVENTORY

BUILDING DATA

    D.   Has tenant paid for any improvements and betterments? _____

           Description _____

           _____

           Value _____

    E.   Is sub-leasing permitted? _____

9.   Is the above property leased from others? _____

    A.   Name and address of Lessor _____

           _____

    B.   Amount of rent _____ Monthly _____ Annual _____

    C.   Term of lease _____ Expiration _____

    D.   Renewal option _____

    E.   Bonus paid for lease _____

    F.   Obligation for building services (heat, janitor, insurance, etc.) _____

           _____

    G.   Current cost of comparable premises _____

10.   Obtain copy of lease agreement. _____

    A.   Abatement provision in event of serious loss or damage _____

           _____

    B.   Are you liable for increase in fire rate on building? _____

    C.   Are you required to carry

                Fire insurance? _____ Amount _____

                Liability insurance? _____ Limits _____

                Plate glass insurance? _____

    D.   Who has control over

                Sprinkler system cut-off valve? _____ _____

                Heating system? _____

                Elevators? _____

I. Do lease provisions make insured responsible for repair or restoration of damage, arising out of its use and occupancy in the following respects: _____

    A.   Damage not resulting from own negligence _____

    B.   All repairs and maintenance other than structural _____

    C.   Structural repairs and/or latent defects _____

    D.   Extraordinary repairs or restoration (upon surrender or otherwise) arising out of perils normally covered by landlord's standard fire insurance policy with extended coverage and vandalism and malicious mischief endorsements, or other casualties beyond reasonable control _____

_____

_____

_____

Yes/No

12. Does the lease expressly deny the tenant's liability in case of "D" above? _____

13. Is landlord required to make all repairs that the tenant is not expressly required to make? _____

14. Does the landlord's fire insurance policy contain a waiver of subrogation clause? _____

15. Does landlord relieve insured in advance of any liability for fire or other casualty losses in excess of payments received from his fire insurance carrier, whether caused by insured's negligence or not? _____

16. Is the lease provision whereunder insured agrees to indemnify and/or hold harmless landlord against landlord's liability for injury or damage to third parties or their property limited (a) "to the extent that it arises out of tenant's use and occupancy" and furthermore, (b) "to the extent that it is not covered by the landlord's negligence or breach of agreement" such as, failure to make repairs for which landlord is responsible? _____

17. Is the lease provision whereunder insured agrees to indemnify and/or hold harmless landlord against damage to the landlord's property limited (a) "to the extent that damage is caused by tenant's negligence" and furthermore, (b) "to be exclusive of damage due to a peril normally covered by landlord's standard fire insurance policy with extended coverage and vandalism and malicious mischief endorsements"? _____

18. Is either (16) or (17) above defined in ambiguous terms such as "in or about" or "on or about" the leased premises, rather than specifically limited to the leased premises? _____

19. Are (16) and (17) above limited to liability "arising out of tenant's use and occupancy"? _____

20. Does any lease provision create directly against insured, as tenant, a liability to any third party other than the landlord? _____

Yes/No

21. Is insured required to indemnify and/or hold harmless the landlord from liability for injury or damage to third parties or their property (a) not caused by insured's negligence, or (b) caused by insured's failure to comply with all provisions of the lease agreement? _____

22. Do you lease, sub-lease, or rent any of the above properties to others? If so, obtain information required in item 9 "B" through "G". _____

23. Building Valuation:

Current replacement value _____

Current "actual cash value" _____

Current "market value" _____

Describe methods of obtaining fire insurance values _____

_____

Cost of excavation _____

Value of foundations and underground wiring and piping (below grade or lowest basement floor) _____

_____

Have previous appraisals been made? _____ By whom? _____

Are values trended? _____ How often? _____

24. Any contemplated alteration, expansion, additions, or demolition? _____

If so, describe, including anticipated starting and completion dates, construction, use, and projected cost.

_____

25. Allowance for debris removal $ _____

26. Does building code affect rebuilding? _____ If so, allowance for demolition $ _____

Allowance for extra cost of construction $ _____

27. Obtain copy of latest fire insurance rate schedule, or authorization to bureau. _____

28. Plate Glass:

Location of all glass (interior and exterior) _____

_____

Type of glass (carrara, brick, bent, vitrolite, etc.) _____

_____

_____

_____

Dimensions of each plate _____

_____

_____

_____

Value of lettering _____

_____

Any neon signs? _____

       Value _____

_____

Any past losses? _____

_____

_____

_____

_____

CLAIM & LOSS HISTORY

Company: _____   Date: _____

A five-year claim and loss history should be developed and maintained on all perils, policies or self-insured exposures. A summary by year may be sufficient if the total number of incidents is excessive. All losses exceeding $10,000 should be itemized and described.

Peril of Policy: **BUILDING DAMAGE**

Date or Year	Location, Description or Claimant	Cause	Uninsured	Insured

CONTENTS DATA

Company: _____   Date: _____

Location: _____

1. Machinery, equipment, tools and dies (including drayage, rigging and installation charges):

    A. Replacement cost new _____

    B. Actual cash value _____

    C. Basis for "B" (Obtain appraisal, if possible.) _____

    _____

    D. Any chattel mortgage _____

    Name _____

    Address _____

2. Furniture and fixtures, equipment and supplies (including drayage, rigging and installation charges):

    A. Replacement cost new _____

    B. Actual cash value _____

    C. Basis for "B" (Obtain appraisal, if available.) _____

    _____

    D. Any chattel mortgage _____

    Name _____

    Address _____

3. Improvements and betterments:

    A. Date installed _____

    B. Original cost _____

    C. Replacement cost _____

    D. Actual cash value _____

    E. Describe (Obtain appraisal, if available.) _____

4. Stock (raw, in process and finished):

   A. Maximum – at cost _____ at selling price _____

   B. Minimum – at cost _____ at selling price _____

   C. Average   – at cost _____ at selling price _____

   D. Present   – at cost _____ at selling price _____

   E. How and when inventoried _____

   _____

   F. Any fluctuations among buildings _____

5. Property of others for repair, processing or other purpose (including goods held on consignment): _____

   _____

6. Value of machinery, materials and stock in hands of processors, sub-contractors, and others. Itemize by
   name, address, description of property, and amount (minimum, maximum, average): _____

   _____

   _____

7. Is there any agreement covering your responsibilities for these values? _____

   _____

8. Property of concessionaires: _____ Consignors _____

9. Employees' belongings: _____

10. Valuable papers or drawings: _____

    A. Value _____ Reproduction cost _____

    B. Where kept _____

    C. Description _____

11. Value of exhibits – sales office: _____

12. Describe type, size and value of signs:

    A. On premises _____

    B. At other locations _____

    _____

13. Care, custody or control problems _____

_____

14. Water damage and sprinkler leakage exposure and percentage of contents value subject to loss: _____

_____

_____

15. Any unusual camera, scientific equipment or valuable instruments: _____

_____

16. Any fine arts in office: _____

17. Any electronic data processing equipment: _____

_____

    A. Who owns them? _____

    B. If leased, who is responsible for damage or destruction? _____

    C. Cost to replace data stored in destroyed unit _____

    D. Potential business interruption or extra expense exposure _____

    E. Any use by others _____

    F. Liability for loss, destruction or misuse of data _____

18. Is stock subject to

    A. Consequential loss? _____

    B. Crime loss? _____

    C. Damage by heat or cold? _____

    D. Spoilage resulting from equipment failure? _____

    E. If any "yes" (A-D), describe, including potential dollar loss. _____

_____

19. Any property under conditional sales agreements? _____ Explain: _____

_____

_____

Appendix
Supplement #26 — 5/76
(Supersedes Supplement #1)

EXPOSURE INVENTORY

CONTENTS DATA

20. Exhibitions:

Value _____

Describe _____

_____

21. Describe (including values) any equipment loaned or rented to others. Get details regarding responsibility for loss or damage. (Obtain copy of agreements.) _____

_____

_____

_____

22. Describe (including values) any equipment loaned or rented from others. Get details regarding responsibility for loss or damage. (Obtain copy of agreements.) _____

_____

_____

_____

CLAIM & LOSS HISTORY

Company: _____   Date: _____

A five-year claim and loss history should be developed and maintained on all perils, policies or self-insured exposures. A summary by year may be sufficient if the total number of incidents is excessive. **All** losses exceeding $10,000 should be itemized and described.

Peril of Policy: **CONTENTS DAMAGE**

Date or Year	Location, Description or Claimant	Cause	Uninsured	Insured

Appendix
Supplement #26 — 5/76
(Supersedes Supplement #1)

National Association of Accountants
Committee on Research
1980-81

Calvin A. Vobroucek
Chairman
Caterpillar Tractor Company
Peoria, Ill.

George Bannon
Bethlehem Steel Corporation
Bethlehem, Pa.

Richard F. Bebee
Alexander Grant & Company
Chicago, Ill.

Robert U. Boehman
North American Products, Inc.
Jasper, Ind.

Germain Boer
Vanderbilt University
Nashville, Tenn.

Paul Dascher
Drexel University
Philadelphia, Pa.

Dwight Davis
A. O. Smith Corporation
Kankakee, Ill.

Paul H. Davis
International Harvester Company
San Diego, Calif.

Geraldine F. Dominiak
Texas Christian University
Fort Worth, Tex.

Patricia P. Douglas
University of Montana
Missoula, Mont.

J. Bernard Eck
May Zima & Company
Daytona Beach, Fla.

Michael L. Ferrante
Ernst & Whinney
White Plains, N.Y.

Penny A. Flugger
Morgan Guaranty Trust Company
New York, N.Y.

Theodore C. Gearhart
GAO-IRS
Washington, D.C.

Charles L. Grant
Becton Dickinson & Company
Rochelle Park, N.J.

John L. Hanson
Electro Corporation
Sarasota, Fla.

John H. Holzapfel
Coopers & Lybrand
Pittsburgh, Pa.

Henry M. Klein
General Instrument
El Paso, Tex.

Ira Landis
Laventhol & Horwath
Los Angeles, Calif.

Paul H. Levine
Magnetic Analysis Corporation
Mt. Vernon, N.Y.

Jack E. Meadows
Combustion Engineering Company
Chattanooga, Tenn.

Thomas J. O'Reilly
Coopers & Lybrand
Cleveland, Ohio

Ronald J. Patten
University of Connecticut
Storrs, Conn.

Howard O. Rockness
Dartmouth College
Hanover, N.H.

W. Peter Salzarulo
Miami University
Oxford, Ohio

Bruce T. Santilli
Tec, Inc.
Tucson, Ariz.

Fred S. Schulte
Tracor, Inc.
Austin, Tex.

Henry A. Schwartz
IBM
Armonk, N.Y.

Milton F. Usry
McIntire School of Commerce
Charlottesville, Va.